Turner's
VENICE

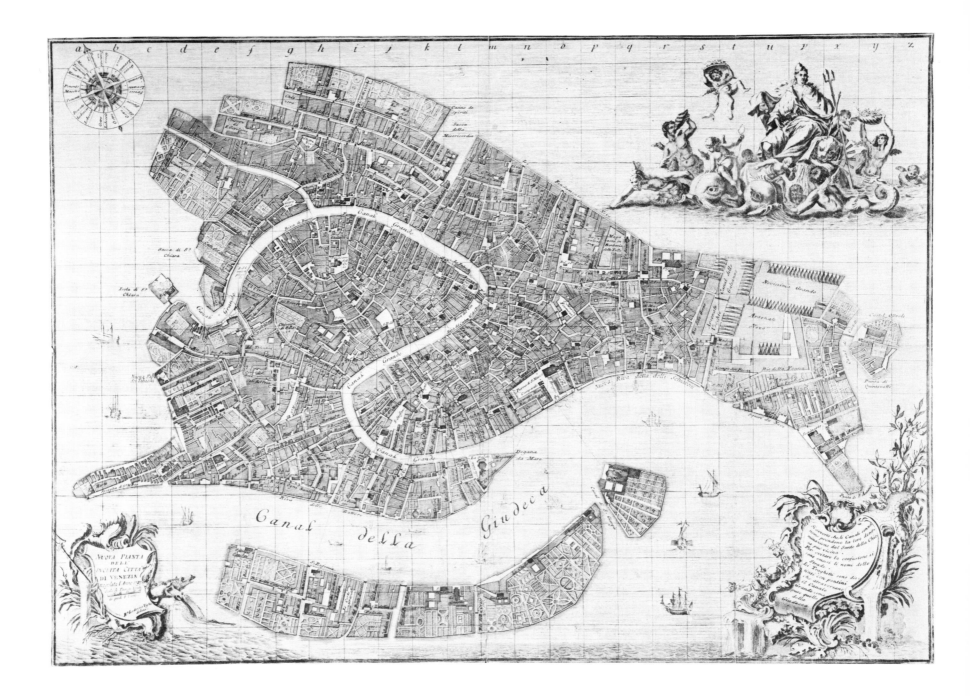

Turner's
VENICE

Lindsay Stainton

PUBLISHED BY
BRITISH MUSEUM PUBLICATIONS
LIMITED

Published by British Museum Publications Limited
46 Bloomsbury Street, London, WC1B 3QQ

British Library Cataloguing in Publication Data
Stainton, Lindsay
   Turner's Venice.
   1. Turner, J.M.W. 2. Venice (Italy) in art
   I. Title
   759.2   ND497.T8
   ISBN 0 7141 8062 9

Frontispiece: *Nuova Pianta dell' Inclita Città di Venezia Regolata l' Anno 1797.*
Engraving. 492 × 660 mm

*The Grand Canal, with S. Maria della Salute. c.*1885. Photograph.
240 × 304 mm. This shows the Grand Canal much as Turner would have
seen it (but as we never see it today), with the water undisturbed by *vaporetti*
and *motoscafi*

Designed by Sebastian Carter

Set in Monophoto Ehrhardt and printed in Great Britain by
Balding + Mansell Limited

Contents

Acknowledgments

The purpose of this book is to make available for the first time a substantial group of Turner's Venetian works in colour reproduction: it is hoped that this selection will bring pleasure to those who love both Turner and Venice. In choosing the plates the emphasis has been put on watercolours as oil paintings have more often been illustrated elsewhere. Invaluable help has been given by my colleagues in the Department of Prints and Drawings, in particular Jenny Bell and Sheila O'Connell. The photography was undertaken with admirable celerity by Stanley Parker-Ross and Ian Jones and the printing with a high regard for quality by Balding + Mansell Limited. At British Museum Publications, Hugh Campbell and Celia Clear were responsible for the initial idea. The text was edited by Emma Myers with the assistance of Suzannah Gough: their efficiency and fortitude put me to shame. I would also like to thank Harriet Bridgeman, Cara Campbell, Sebastian Carter, Ann Forsdyke, J.A. Gere, Evelyn Joll, J.G. Links, Mary Lutyens, John Nicoll, Viola Pemberton-Pigott, Nicholas Russell, Chris Shone and Andrew Wilton. The introduction owes much to Michael Kitson, whose criticism was invaluable. He also patiently discussed problems of dating and topography and saved me from several errors.

Since this book first went to press, Peter Bicknell has most kindly drawn my attention to a hitherto unnoticed reference in a journal kept by his ancestress Christine, the daughter-in-law of Turner's patron, Elhanan Bicknell. On 24 June 1845 she wrote: 'Pleasant party [at Herne Hill]. My Father, Turner, Etty, Webster, Denning – grand discussion on duelling. My Father the only one who defended it! . . . Turner going to Venice' (ms. in the National Library of Scotland). There is, however, no other evidence that Turner visited Venice after 1840.

All photographs except those listed below are © British Museum Publications Ltd 1985 and were taken by Stanley Parker-Ross and Ian Jones. The author and publishers are grateful to the following for permission to reproduce photographs:

Ashmolean Museum, Oxford pls 69, 91, 93. The Trustees of The British Museum Frontispiece, figs 1, 2, 3, 4, 8, 9, 11, 16, pl. 109. Conway Library, Courtauld Institute of Art, London figs 17, 19. The Syndics of The Fitzwilliam Museum, Cambridge pls 68, 86. Henry E. Huntington Library & Art Gallery, California fig. 12. National Gallery of Ireland, Dublin pls 76, 80, 90. The Trustees of The National Gallery, London pl. 106. National Galleries of Scotland, Edinburgh pls 88, 89, 92, 95, 108. National Trust (photo: The Bridgeman Art Library) pl. 111. National Museum of Wales, Cardiff (photo: Robert Harding Picture Library) pl. 112. Private Collections pl. 94; figs 6, 13, 14. The Earl of Shelburne fig. 7. Sotheby Parke Bernet Inc. pl. 110. Tate Gallery, London pls 96, 99, 101, 103–5; fig. 10. Toledo Museum of Art, Ohio pl. 102. The Board of Trustees of The Victoria & Albert Museum, London pl. 100. The Trustees of The Wallace Collection, London pl. 107; fig. 15. Witt Library, Courtauld Institute of Art, London figs 7, 18. York City Art Gallery fig. 5.

Introduction

When Turner arrived for the first time in Venice for a short stay in September 1819, the city was passing through the most disastrous period in its history. But it was this very period that inspired the Romantic conception of Venice which has endured in some respects to this day.

Following almost three centuries of slow decline (which can be traced back to the fall of Constantinople in 1453 and to the gradual loss of the monopoly of trade with the East), the final extinction of the 1100-year old Republic in 1797 was a crushing humiliation and the prelude to much suffering. In the previous year, Napoleon Bonaparte had chased an Austrian army out of Lombardy, overrun part of the Venetian mainland (the Veneto) and demanded the overthrow of the ancient Venetian constitution. The *Signoria*, without allies or armed forces of its own, had no choice but to submit. On 12 May, 1797, the Great Council voted itself out of existence and agreed to the formation of an elected municipality; the last Doge, Ludovico Manin, resigned; and French troops entered the city. But this was only the beginning. By the Treaty of Campo Formio a few months later, Venice and the Veneto were handed over to the Austrians in return for their recognition of the French-dominated 'Cisalpine Republic' of Lombardy and Emilia-Romagna; then, after Austria's defeat at Austerlitz in 1805, the territories were seized back by Napoleon and absorbed into his new Kingdom of Italy.

The citizens were too enervated either to rejoice or to protest.

Already in 1797, great quantities of pictures, sculptures, church plate and other works of art, including the bronze horses of St Mark's, had been looted and removed to Paris (though most were to be returned after Waterloo). The renewed French occupation brought changes typical of Napoleonic administrations everywhere. Many monasteries and churches were suppressed, public gardens were opened, a few buildings were given neo-classical alterations and the Academy of Fine Arts was rehoused in the former convent of the Carità (where it is today). Such efforts at modernisation were, however, undermined by the imposition of heavy taxes and the neglect of the economy. Not surprisingly therefore, when the Austrians retook Venice after a prolonged siege in 1814, they found the city 'partly deserted and ruinous.'[1] Much trade had been lost to Trieste. The fleet was incapable of putting to sea. Between 1797 and 1824, the population of the six *sestieri* (i.e. the central 'sixths' of Venice, without the outlying islands) fell from 137,240 to 113,827 and the number of workers in the Arsenal from 3,302 to 773.

In 1815, at the Congress of Vienna, the territories of Lombardy, Venice and the Veneto were annexed to the Austrian Empire and, apart from the seventeen months of revolutionary government headed by Daniele Manin in Venice in 1848–9, they remained so constituted until allowed to join the newly independent Kingdom of Italy in 1866. At first, Austrian rule was welcomed by the Venetians as it promised to bring peace and stability – a promise that was for the most part fulfilled.

Programmes of relief and public works were carried out, especially in the three or four years after 1814 when there was a succession of poor harvests on the mainland. Within the city, although some buildings were pulled down, others were repaired: for example, the Campanile of St Mark's was under restoration in 1819–22 and again in 1839–40, both, as it happens, periods during which Turner visited Venice.[2] On the other hand, the Austrian administration was politically and economically repressive and grotesquely cumbersome.

However, as under the French, it was taxation that was the most onerous feature of Austrian rule. The Austrians took far more out of their North Italian provinces than they put into them. In the 1820s and 1830s, these provinces furnished a quarter of the revenues of the Austrian Empire. At the same time, manufacturing industry was discouraged from competing with Austrian-made goods. In Venice, the traditional trades of ship-building and silk-weaving were never properly revived and the only industry that flourished was the manufacture of glassware. Commerce, banking and such manufacturing as existed were now dominated by the bourgeoisie though the nobility, which had been rendered powerless by the French, recovered some of its influence in society. The petite bourgeoisie made their living as shopkeepers, hoteliers and so on, serving the tourist trade which gradually revived. Even more than today, the water governed the lives of ordinary Venetians. Small and medium-sized vessels, ranging from fishing-boats with brightly painted sails and small barges to humble rowing dinghies, either moored to the quays or floating motionless in clusters on the Grand Canal and Bacino di San Marco, were the most conspicuous feature of Venice after the architecture. In addition, weaving their way swiftly round the stationary boats, were the slim black gondolas, compared by Shelley in a wonderful phrase to 'moths of which a coffin might have been the chrysalis'.[3]

Such, then, was the Venice that Turner saw for the first time on that September day in 1819, when he stepped ashore from the gondola that had brought him across the Lagoon from the mainland at Fusina. The city he encountered was, it is true, partly decayed, economically backward, and dejected in spirit from the continued presence of a foreign power. Nevertheless, like all sensitive travellers – and who, visually, was more sensitive than Turner? – he would have been struck by the astonishing picturesqueness of the place, the unending combinations of shapes which its varied buildings presented to the eye and, above all, by the incomparable setting of the city between sea and sky. He was well equipped by his earlier experience to appreciate and record these things, as we shall see. In addition, he is likely to have come furnished with some preconceived emotional attitudes to the city and some notion of its historical significance as well as its contemporary condition. From time immemorial, Venice had aroused strong feelings in those who visited it. With the fall of the Republic and the rise of the Romantic movement in Europe, these feelings took on a new, more complex and more elegiac form. This was especially the case with literary-minded visitors from Britain, who, by their writings, largely created the Romantic response to Venice. Turner would have absorbed something of their attitudes, and, even if his drawings and watercolours of 1819 are too slight to show it, his later, more ambitious Venetian works are redolent of the brilliant light, dream-like atmosphere and insubstantial splendours which haunted writers such as Beckford, the historian John Moore, Samuel Rogers, Lady Morgan, Shelley, Byron and, for a time, Ruskin.[4]

Of these Turner had most in common with Byron.[5] Byron's vigour, his rhetoric, his speed of thought and poetic composition all have their equivalents in Turner's creative procedures, as does his ability simultaneously to express appreciative and hostile feelings. Like Byron, Turner had no systematic philosophy but responded to scenes and events from the centre of his own powerful instincts. Both men were earthy yet capable of the highest flights of fantasy. They were equally skilled in using both the simplest and the most complex technical forms. Moreover, both were conscious of their roots in the eighteenth century. They shared that century's assumption that art and literature should be concerned with ideas – an attitude that Turner maintained long after it had ceased to appeal to most other British painters or their public. Of course, there were differences between them, partly arising from their different social origins. Byron was aristocratic and at ease in fashionable society; he could afford to put his genius into his life as well as into his art and ultimately to throw away both. Turner, humbly born and shy except when among close friends and fellow artists, husbanded his time carefully and kept his irregular private life concealed. Lacking Byron's educational as well as social advantages, he had to acquire his wide, if sometimes erratic, knowledge of literature, history and science for himself.

Nevertheless, the affinity between them is striking and Byron was one of the few contemporary poets whose works Turner certainly knew. He had already used a quotation from the third canto of *Childe Harold's Pilgrimage* to accompany the title of his painting, *The Field of Waterloo* in the Royal Academy catalogue for 1818,[6] and he probably read the fourth canto on its appearance the same year. This canto includes the famous stanzas on Venice. Familiar though these are, three are worth quoting as they not only provide a valuable introduction to Turner but also sum up the Romantic attitude to the city:

> I stood in Venice, on the Bridge of Sighs;
> A palace and a prison on each hand:
> I saw from out the wave her structures rise
> As from the stroke of the enchanter's wand:
> A thousand years their cloudy wings expand
> Around me, and a dying Glory smiles
> O'er the far times, when many a subject land
> Look'd to the wingèd Lion's marble piles,
> Where Venice sate in state, throned on her hundred isles!...

> In Venice Tasso's echoes are no more,
> And silent rows the songless gondolier;
> Her palaces are crumbling to the shore,
> And music meets not always now the ear:
> Those days are gone – but Beauty still is here.
> States fall, arts fade – but Nature doth not die.
> Nor yet forget how Venice once was dear,
> The pleasant place of all festivity,
> The revel of the earth, the masque of Italy!...

> I loved her from my boyhood; she to me
> Was as a fairy city of the heart,
> Rising like water-columns from the sea,
> Of joy the sojourn, and of wealth the mart;
> And Otway, Radcliffe, Schiller, Shakespeare's art,
> Had stamp'd her image in me, and even so,
> Although I found her thus, we did not part;
> Perchance even dearer in her day of woe,
> Than when she was a boast, a marvel, and a show.

Here, nature is brought together with art, amazement with regret, splendour with decay. Everything is evoked as in a dazzle of airy light. The imagery is shifting, fluid, reminiscent of the way in which forms and light dissolve into their reflections in Turner's paintings. Even the literary references have their counterpart in Turner, who in Venice thought constantly of Shakespeare. But the question remains, was Turner's Venice a city of beauty and a source of delight as Ruskin claimed on his behalf? Or was it rather a symbol of decline and death, as the lines attached to *The Sun of Venice going to Sea* imply?: '... Nor heeds the demon that in grim repose / Expects his evening prey.'. The answer suggested by the comparison with Byron is 'something of both'.

To the Romantics, as afterwards to Ruskin in *The Stones of Venice*, the significance of Venice was poetic and, as it were, 'public'. The city's history and its eventual fate had a meaning for contemporary Europe, especially Britain. This contrasts with the attitude both of the eighteenth century and of later periods. The eighteenth century was moved in its response to Venice chiefly by curiosity; in the visual field its thirst for information was satisfied by the brilliantly detailed paintings of Canaletto. In the late nineteenth and early twentieth centuries, feelings were no less intense but were more introspective; instead of trying to reach some sort of judgement about the city and to draw lessons from it, a writer such as Henry James was preoccupied with analysing and describing his own impressions. In the intervening Romantic period, Venice was a city of the mind and heart as well as of the eye. It aroused passions and thoughts. It was also not quite real. The light and the water worked a magic on it that bemused the spectator. Veiled in mist, reddened by the setting sun or made ghostly by moonlight, the city could easily be imagined as it was in its days of greatness. The present conjured up the past, rendering the two not wholly distinct. It was this Venice that was painted by Turner.

In one respect, however, there had been, at the time of his arrival, no change since the eighteenth century. This was in the attitude towards Venice as a work of art, meaning by that both the pictorial representation of the city and the critical assessment of Venetian architecture. It was generally agreed that Venice as a whole was a magnificent spectacle, but only buildings in the classical style, particularly if they were designed by Palladio, were individually worthy of respect. Byzantine and Gothic buildings, such as St Mark's and the Ducal Palace, were considered at best quaint and at worst barbarous. The view expressed by Gibbon in 1765 – that 'the spectacle of Venice afforded some hours of astonishment' but that 'the centre of the city was a large square decorated with the worst architecture I ever saw'[7] – was hardly modified sixty years later. There is no reason to suppose that Turner's opinion differed from that of everyone else at the time. Certainly his paintings and watercolours tend to be designed round such buildings as the Palladian S. Giorgio Maggiore, the baroque church of S. Maria della Salute and the Renaissance and Baroque palaces on the Grand Canal. The one earlier monument that he uses frequently is the Campanile of St Mark's (which is Romanesque and thus 'honorary' Renaissance, with an actual Renaissance pinnacle). Byzantine and Gothic buildings are not neglected in his work, but are less clearly defined. It was not until the 1830s, by which time Turner's taste was long-established, that the medieval churches and palaces of Venice began to be appreciated for their own sakes; and not until the appearance of Ruskin's *Stones of Venice* in 1851–53 that they came to be seen as great architecture and the expression of the deepest instincts of the Venetian people.[8]

Canaletto's paintings dominated the pictorial interpretation of the city for almost as long a period. These paintings, together with the engravings after them and the artist's own etchings (plate 106; fig. 18), were so successful in creating and perpetuating the image of Venice as visitors wished to remember it, that no other method seemed necessary or indeed possible. Well into the Romantic age visitors continued to say that the works of Canaletto (who had died in 1768) and his followers had so familiarised them with the city that they felt they had seen it before they got there. That so objective and precise a rendering as Canaletto's should still have been thought appropriate in the Romantic period is not a little surprising, given the nature of the literary response by this date.

Canaletto's success also ensured that Venetian view-painting remained a monopoly of local artists. Leaving aside the special case of Guardi (who was less literal in his approach and perhaps for that reason less popular with British patrons), minor painters such as Giuseppe Borsato and Giovanni Migliara continued until the 1830s to turn out views of Venice in a debased version of Canaletto's style. Very few British landscape painters had bothered to visit the city during the eighteenth century and between 1797 and 1815 they were, of course, unable to do so even if they had wanted to. Apart from Reynolds the only two artists of note to visit Venice were Richard Wilson, who executed some half-a-dozen slight drawings of the city during his stay in 1751, and John Robert Cozens who stopped there for a few days with William Beckford in 1782 and so far as we know made just one.[9] So little did Venice, by comparison with Central and Southern Italy, attract British eighteenth-century artists that the otherwise fairly comprehensive publication, *Select Views in Italy* (1792–6), containing engravings after John 'Warwick' Smith, William Byrne and John Emes, includes not a single Venetian view. To Turner, Bonington, Clarkson Stanfield and others, who began producing oil paintings of Venice in the late 1820s and early 1830s, the tradition of Canaletto was still alive, and they took this tradition as their starting point.

Exceptionally, however, Turner's work produced in and around 1819 owed little to Canaletto. For one thing, he made no oil paintings of Venice during this period; or rather, he executed only a single large canvas begun after his return and not carried beyond the stage of underpainting.[10] He also executed a few finished watercolours, some painted before he saw Venice and others after his return home. In these the influence of Canaletto is only marginally relevant. While actually in Venice, Turner confined himself, as was his habit when touring, to pencil drawings and watercolour sketches which sprang from the very different tradition established by himself and other English watercolourists while working in their own country. The drawings and sketches made by Turner on this occasion were also unusual in two other, contrasting respects. On the one hand, they constituted a larger and more interesting body of work than that previously executed in Venice by any British artist. On the other hand, this group of approximately 135 pencil sketches and four watercolours was small by Turner's standards and represented only a fraction of the number he went on to produce in other parts of Italy. Indeed, in the context of his 1819–20 visit to Italy as a whole, it is clear that Venice was hardly more than a stopping place on the way to Rome, which was the real object of his journey. He seems to have stayed in Venice for at most five days, whereas he was in Rome (including an excursion of about a fortnight to Naples) for nearly three months.

That Turner should have wanted above all to visit Rome at this stage in his career is understandable. The Napoleonic wars had prevented him from going earlier, and commissions and other obligations delayed him for a further few years. 1819 was, it seems, the first year in which he was free. By this time, his friends Lawrence and Eastlake were in Rome, the former writing back to England urging him to join them. More important was the fact that much of his work almost from the beginning of his career had been orientated towards Rome and its surrounding countryside. Claude Lorrain, Richard Wilson and John Robert Cozens – three artists who each in his own way profoundly influenced Turner – all found their main source of inspiration there; and many of Turner's ideal landscapes had been based at second hand on Italian views. His early patron, Sir Richard Colt Hoare, had already introduced him to the pleasures of classical archaeology,[11] and he had taught himself the rudiments of Roman history.

Turner's motives for visiting Rome are thus easily explained.

What drew him to Venice? Given the lack of concern with the city on the part of earlier British painters and the absence of any anticipatory signs of interest in his previous career, he might easily have omitted it altogether from his itinerary. One possible reason is the fourth canto of *Childe Harold's Pilgrimage* with its stanzas on Venice preceding those on Rome; as already mentioned, Turner had probably read this canto on its first appearance in 1818. Another more certain if more prosaic reason was his involvement in James Hakewill's *Picturesque Tour of Italy*.[12] In 1816–17 Hakewill made over 300 pencil drawings of Italian scenery as the basis for a series of engravings to be published together with a short descriptive text. The engravers were to work, however, not from Hakewill's rather thin though careful drawings (probably executed with the aid of a *camera lucida*) but from finished watercolours worked up from them by professional artists – a procedure common in the period and one of which Turner already had personal experience. On 15 June 1818, Turner was paid 200 guineas for ten watercolours to be used for this series, and a memorandum dated a month later shows that he had been commissioned to execute a further ten. An additional 40 were commissioned from various other artists, and it seems that all 60 watercolours were finished or nearly finished by mid-July 1818. In the event, only thirty-six engravings, of which exactly half were after Turner, were issued in groups of four or five between 1818 and 1820, and in 1820 the series was re-published as a book. One of Turner's engraved watercolours is *A View of the Rialto from the South* (see note to plate 60), and one of those not engraved is of *The Custom House (Dogana) & Church of the Madonna della Salute, at the entrance of the Grand Canal*.[13] Both are now untraced, but the general appearance of the former, if not its colour and handling, can be gathered from the engraving (fig. 1), while some idea of the latter can be deduced from Hakewill's drawing. The size, 140×216 mm, was comparatively small for finished watercolours by Turner at this date.

Not surprisingly, the Rialto was painted several times by Canaletto from various viewpoints, but even in the composition (one of two versions of which is at Woburn) closest to

1. John Pye after J.M.W. Turner, *The Rialto*. 1820. Engraving. 220 × 143 mm. Published in Hakewill's *Picturesque Tour of Italy*, 1818–20 (R.144)

Hakewill/Turner the Italian artist imagined himself standing further away from the bridge and he characteristically broadened out the space. In constricting the space both laterally and in depth, Hakewill/Turner show the buildings closer to one another and crowding in upon the Grand Canal, as they do in reality. As might be expected of a strictly topographical composition, the treatment of detail is thorough and minute if (in the engraving at least) somewhat mechanical. Compared with Turner's later, independent, work, this view of the Rialto is pedantic and stiff, but he did his best to enliven the effect by the disposition of light and shade, by the pattern of sails and curved awnings on the boats in the middle distance, and by the figures, which were entirely his invention: there are none in Hakewill's drawings.

The significance of Turner's association with Hakewill for his first visit to Italy did not end there. The proportion of Venetian scenes in *A Picturesque Tour* to views elsewhere in the country – two out of sixty in the original scheme, one out of thirty-six in the published version – was echoed in his own itinerary. What is more, Hakewill supplied Turner with detailed notes for his journey, including information about costs and distances, and advice on where to stay and on places and pictures to see, all neatly written out in a notebook which the artist took with him.[14] The only variation is that, while Hakewill assumed that Turner would begin at Milan, perhaps under the influence of J.C. Eustace's *A Tour through Italy* of 1813 (a book from which the artist himself took notes),[15] Turner in fact began his journey with Venice, and the same arrangement was eventually adopted when Hakewill's *A Picturesque Tour of Italy* was issued as a book. Turner also copied into one of his sketchbooks[16] over 70 engravings from Smith, Byrne and Emes's *Select Views in Italy*, so it can be seen that he prepared himself with great thoroughness for his first Italian tour. Although he could easily have left Venice out, it seems clear that he planned from the start to go there, even at the cost of a deviation of several hundred miles from the direct route from Milan to Bologna which he might otherwise have taken.

On 31 July 1819, aged forty-four, Turner left London for the

Continent.[17] As he had done in 1802 he travelled by way of Dover, Calais and Paris to Lyons, then took the road through Chambéry and Modane and over the Mont-Cenis Pass to Turin and Milan. His sketches establish his itinerary, though they are few and far between until he reached the Alps. From Milan, he made an excursion to the Italian Lakes (Como, Lugano and Maggiore), seemingly going as far as the Simplon Pass over which a new road had been constructed by French engineers in 1807.[18] Once among lakes and mountains, a type of scenery that he had scarcely experienced since his visit to Switzerland in 1802, he lingered. Many rapidly executed pencil sketches record his delight in the mountains, and he also made his first watercolour of an Italian subject, a *View of Lake Como* (plate 1). However, he did not neglect cities, and drawings exist in his sketchbooks of several of the principal Renaissance and Baroque buildings in Turin, Milan and Brescia and the other towns on the way to Venice. He reached Venice, if the name appearing in the *Gazzetta Privilegiata di Venezia* has been correctly identified as his ('Turner William, gent. inglese' – arrived from Milan), on 8 or 9 September. According to the same newspaper, which supposedly listed the arrival and departure of all visitors to Venice, he left on 12 or 13 September. Something will be said later about the reliability of these lists as a source of information for Turner's visits (they were usefully brought to light in this context by Hardy George)[19] but for the 1819 visit they can probably be relied upon, if only because they agree with other evidence. The given dates mean that Turner was in the city for at most five and possibly as little as three days. At first sight this seems almost incredible, bearing in mind the number of drawings he made in Venice, but it can be explained by the speed at which he habitually worked and by the fact that the range of his activity was narrower than it seems.

Turner is likely to have taken Hakewill's advice and put up at the Leone Bianco, a hotel situated on the San Marco side of the Grand Canal, below the Rialto Bridge and just out of sight in the engraving shown here as fig. 1. For pencil sketches, he used parts of two sketchbooks of almost identical size: TB CLXXV, *Milan to Venice* (112 × 189 mm) and TB CLXXVI, *Venice to Ancona*

(112 × 187 mm). He drew on both sides of the paper and often across the width of two leaves, while on some pages there is more than one sketch. The first 35 or so sheets and the last sheet of the first sketchbook are filled with sketches of Milan and other places between there and Venice; the remaining 54 sheets contain between them 80 sketches of Venice itself. He filled the first twenty sheets of the second sketchbook in Venice, and the remaining sixty-eight on the way south, through Bologna to Rimini and eventually Ancona.

Contrary to what has sometimes been supposed, it appears that Turner's method of working in Venice was really very simple. Starting from the Leone Bianco, he had himself rowed in a gondola up the Grand Canal as far as the mouth of the Canale di Cannaregio, where he got out his first sketchbook (TB CLXXV), opening it at the last page but one, i.e. after the single sheet at the end containing sketches of Milan. He then continued upstream, sketching as he went S. Geremia, the Palazzo Labia, the Scalzi and S. Simeone Piccolo, and, along the way, numerous small boats. When he reached S. Lucia (demolished in 1860 to make way for the railway station) he turned round and started back, but did not begin sketching again until he was in sight of the Rialto Bridge. Here he produced a flurry of sketches, prompted no doubt by the fame of the bridge and the fact that he had earlier depicted it for Hakewill. He drew the bridge from both sides and also views past it into the recesses of the city. Then followed sketches of some of the palaces (Rezzonico, Balbi, Garzoni, Grassi, etc.; these are seen looking upstream in fig. 2) on the lower reaches of the Canal, with campanili, sometimes quite distant ones, rising up behind them. Finally he arrived near the mouth of the Grand Canal, with the massive Palazzo Corner della Ca'Grande framing the composition on the left and the church of S. Maria della Salute on the right; this was to be a favourite view in his later watercolours. After that Turner would have found himself on the open water of the Bacino di San Marco surrounded by all the famous monuments: the Dogana, S. Giorgio Maggiore (fig. 3), the Piazzetta, the Ducal Palace, the Campanile of St Mark's and so on. A view in this area had already been the subject of his second watercolour developed from a drawing by Hakewill. Here he made a large number of pencil sketches. As already mentioned, the Campanile was under repair in 1819 and had a small platform at the very top for the renewal of the angel; this platform seems to be visible in some of the sketches executed during this visit.

Turner's trip down the Grand Canal was not as continuous as this simple account suggests. It is clear that from time to time he looked back (as in fig. 2) and sometimes doubled back or even went ashore. He seems also to have missed out some pages and filled them in later, since the sequence of buildings in the sketchbook does not always correspond with their actual order on the Canal. He must have gone ashore at least once, for there is a sketch of the Arsenal and another of a detail of Titian's *St Peter Martyr* in the church of SS. Giovanni e Paolo. In accordance with Hakewill's advice, he sketched a few other pictures in palaces and churches, including Veronese's *Family of Darius before Alexander*, at that time in the Palazzo Pisani, now in the National Gallery, London.[20] He could just have done all this, including the 80 drawings in the sketchbook, in a single day, and certainly in two. Some of these drawings, such as that in fig. 2, are very elaborate and must have taken some time to execute, but others are so slight that they could have been done in a few minutes.

The other sketchbook (TB CLXXVI) is similar in character though it covers somewhat different ground. More than half the 20 or so Venetian sketches in it are taken from different points along the Molo and the Riva degli Schiavoni, looking in various directions. In a few cases (fig. 3), Turner gazes out beyond Venice to the mainland, or possibly the Lido, and studies the sky. Other sketches show that he went to the Giudecca and sketched S. Maria della Salute and the Dogana from the rear, with the Campanile of St Mark's and the Ducal Palace beyond them.

As on his earlier tours in Britain and abroad, Turner used his pencil in Venice in 1819 to amass detailed records of the city for possible use in finished work later. Given his powers of observation and his great manual dexterity, the method he devised was the most efficient possible. His hand flows over the paper, defining roof-lines, situating objects in pictorial space, recreating the recession of the buildings as they follow the Grand Canal and putting in sufficient detail for his purposes – which sometimes meant drawing only a few windows in a façade with any precision, leaving the rest to be reconstituted from memory. It suited Turner's style that most Venetian buildings have their bases hidden in water rather than resting visibly on firm ground. He was an artist for whom the visual characteristics of an object were always suggested more by its contour than by any complete description of its form or by its exact position on a hypothetical ground-plan. The eye could fill in for itself where the object – be it a building, tree or mountain – sprang from, while the contour suggested the play of light and the movement of air. Of no pencil drawings by Turner is this more true than of the sketches of Venice that he made in 1819. Vivacity is their keynote. Not only do they capture the sensation of Venetian light, but their occasional colour notes are on the verge of suggesting Venetian colour as well.

Once colour itself was added, the sensation of light and atmosphere became even more vivid. We see this in the four watercolour views reproduced on plates 2–5, which are by far the most remarkable product of Turner's visit to Venice in 1819, certainly more so than the finished watercolours executed on his return. The quality of these watercolour views – or sketches, as they should properly be termed – is outstanding, and was in a sense the result of accident. Ruskin claimed that Venice helped to release Turner's imagination: 'there he found freedom of space, brilliancy of light, variety of colour, massy simplicity of general form; and to Venice we owe many of the motives in which his highest powers of colour have been displayed after that change in his system of which we should now take note'.[21] Ruskin was, however, referring to Turner's Venetian experiences in the 1830s and 1840, not to the visit of 1819, of which he knew nothing at the time when he wrote this passage; and, illuminating though the comment is in a general sense, it would be more correct to say that the 1819 sketches owed as much to what Turner brought to Venice as to what he derived from her. His first Venetian watercolours would not have been what they are without Girtin's *White House*, or John Robert Cozens's

2. (*above*) J.M.W. Turner, *The Grand Canal.* 1819. Pencil. 110 × 370 mm
(TB CLXXV-71a, 72)

3. (*right*) J.M.W. Turner, *S. Giorgio Maggiore*, 1819. Pencil. 113 × 186 mm
(TB CLXXVI-21)

earlier, serene and delicately atmospheric views of the Bay of Naples and Isola Bella on Lago Maggiore; nor without Turner's study of Claude, and his experiments with the use of a high colour key in his own work during the two or three years before his departure for Italy. In seeking to explain the miracle of the four Venetian watercolour sketches, it might be fairest to say that the distinctive characteristics of Venice were the catalyst that released Turner's innate qualities as an artist and enabled him to achieve hitherto undreamt of expression – which, perhaps, is what Ruskin is half-suggesting.

To speak of the miracle of these sketches is hardly an exaggeration. In subtlety of effect combined with economy of means they are unsurpassed in Turner's work. He had never before used such pure or transparent colour for such naturalistic purposes. No previous artist had attempted to paint the effect of Venetian buildings veiled in mist or partly dissolved by the glare of sunlight, or seen from a distance at sunrise or sunset. The prismatic colours in the sky in *Looking east from the Giudecca: early morning* (?) (plate 4) show Turner breaking new ground. The colours he employs are the 'aerial' ones to which he refers in his lectures on perspective; those seen when white light is transmitted through a prism, as distinct from the local colours inherent in objects. By placing some dabs of red – a colour which comes forward – in the centre and surrounding them with washes of blue, a recessive colour, and yellow, which is spatially neutral, Turner creates a colour composition both on the surface and in depth that anticipates his late unfinished oil painting, *Norham Castle*.

A few words should be said about the technical method by which these watercolours were produced. Along with the view of *Lake Como* (plate 1) and some half-a-dozen unidentifiable 'colour beginnings', they come from a sketchbook measuring 225×288 mm, the remaining sheets of which were left blank.[22] The question is whether or not they were executed directly from nature. *S. Giorgio Maggiore* (plate 2) and *The Punta della Salute, with the Zitelle in the distance* (plate 3) are clearly taken from the same viewpoint close to the Palazzo Giustiniani (later the Hotel Europa where Turner stayed on his subsequent visits), and if

these were placed side by side they would form a continuous panorama. The fall of the light shows that they were also executed in rapid succession, in the early morning. So closely does the treatment of light accord with the buildings when they are seen from this viewpoint that it is difficult to believe that either watercolour could have been executed *except* from nature. Plate 4, on the other hand, though closely similar in style, is topographically less exact and seems to be an imaginary view, in which a sunrise or sunset over the Lagoon is recreated and combined with an impression of the silhouette of Venice seen on arrival or departure. Plate 5, showing the Campanile and Ducal Palace across the Bacino from the direction of S. Giorgio Maggiore, is of yet another kind, being the only one of the four that is based on a pencil outline; and while the outline may have been drawn from nature, the colour, which is more abstract and less descriptive than in the others, could be a later addition.

These four watercolours, though superficially very much alike, thus appear to have been produced in three quite different ways. If this analysis is correct, it follows that there is no reliable method by which Turner's Venetian watercolours can be clearly divided into those directly executed from nature and those worked up from memory or on the basis of sketches. This conclusion applies equally to the much greater number of watercolours produced during his second and third visits. The most one can do is to make an intelligent guess. The closeness with which we can follow Turner's creative procedure in his pencil drawings makes the uncertainty concerning the way in which his watercolours were produced all the more tantalising. But the fact that different methods could sometimes yield identical results is itself revealing.

On 12 or 13 September Turner left Venice to go south down the Adriatic coast to Ancona, and thence to Rome. He was now in a very different country and wrote of the road from Loreto to Recanati, 'Color of the hills Wilson Claude . . .'.[23] He reached Rome at the beginning of October and remained until the end of the year, returning through Tuscany and again over the Mont Cenis Pass to arrive in London on 1 February 1820. He had filled some twenty sketchbooks with a total of approximately 1500

4. J.M.W. Turner, *The Grand Canal, looking towards the Rialto*. 1819. Pencil. 111 × 375 mm (TB CLXXV-48a, 49)

drawings, of which fifty to sixty were watercolours, all but six or so views of Rome or Naples. On the following day he met the diarist, Joseph Farington, who recorded him saying, 'Tivoli, Venice, Albano – Terni – fine'. Despite all he had seen in Central and Southern Italy, Venice remained in Turner's memory; and although Rome and the mythology of the ancient world occupied a large part of his mind for the next dozen years, he continued to paint Venetian subjects at least at the beginning of this period.

One was the already mentioned oil painting, *The Rialto, Venice*, which was apparently intended as a companion to *Rome from the Vatican*[24], but never finished. A watercolour similar to it in composition, likewise unfinished, is now in the National Gallery of Ireland.[25] Three finished watercolours also belong to this time: a view of S. Maria della Salute from the Campo della Carità,[26] and two Venetian subjects which form part of a small series of views in Italy executed for the artist's old friend and patron, Walter Fawkes.[27] One of these, *The Rialto*, was an enlarged version of the composition originally made for Hakewill's *Picturesque Tour of Italy*. Turner had now seen and sketched this subject for himself (fig. 4), and had chosen a viewpoint further away from the bridge and nearer the water level. The effect was even more crowded than in the Hakewill view, and also more animated and more imposing. To the patron it would still have been intelligible in terms of Canaletto, but with modifications of style that brought this approach up to date. The second watercolour for Fawkes, inscribed *Venice from Fusina* and dated 1821, is unusual in showing a scene that for some reason had been omitted from the traditional iconography of Venetian view painting, though it was part of the experience of every visitor. Boats, gondoliers and waiting travellers with their baggage are disposed across the foreground, just as their equivalents are in Turner's paintings of English beach scenes

5. (*left*) William Etty, *The Bridge of Sighs*. R.A. 1835. Oil on canvas.
80 × 50.8 cm. City Art Gallery, York

6. (*above*) Samuel Prout, *The Ducal Palace, Venice*. R.A. 1826. Watercolour.
724 × 1117 mm. Private Collection

and Swiss lakes. In the background, on the far side of a darkened lagoon, Venice lies illuminated by the light of the setting sun, whose rays streak the clouds with red and gold.

While Turner was giving his mind to other subjects, more British painters were going to Venice. In November 1822, William Etty (1787–1849) arrived, fell head-over-heels in love with the city ('Venice, dear Venice! thy pictured glories haunt my fancy now!') and stayed for seven months.[28] He was primarily a figure painter and not a landscapist, and he made few sketches of outdoor scenes; among these, however, were the two studies on which he based his oil painting, *The Bridge of Sighs* (fig. 5)[29] exhibited in 1835. He spent most of his time in the Accademia, painting human figures from the life and copying Venetian Renaissance pictures in oil colours – the first British artist known to have done so in Venice itself. In 1824, he was followed by the watercolourist, Samuel Prout (1783–1852), who also remained for some months and, as Ruskin somewhat exaggeratedly put it, made Venice 'peculiarly his own'. It was Prout, not Turner, who introduced Ruskin to Venetian architecture. His 'reed pen outline and peculiar touch' were, thought the critic, 'the only means of expressing the crumbling character of stone.'[30] As this comment suggests, Prout's approach was more literally descriptive than Turner's and he was also more at home with the Gothic, which Ruskin preferred and in which Prout came later to specialise. In 1825, Prout sent four Venetian watercolours to the Old Water Colour Society Exhibition – the first views of Venice by a British artist to be publicly shown. These were followed in 1826 by his very large watercolour, *The Ducal Palace, Venice* (fig. 6), exhibited at the Royal Academy, a ponderous and not altogether typical work still dependent in composition, if not in style, on the paintings of Canaletto. Prout later abandoned this approach in favour of close-up views and interior scenes; he came finally to depict Venice as Ruskin saw it, as a city of dark passage-ways, encrusted surfaces and massive stones.

1826 was also the year in which Bonington (1802–28) visited Venice for a four-week stay in the company of his patron, Baron Rivet. After Turner, Bonington was the most notable interpreter of Venice in terms of painting until the arrival of Monet. Like Etty, he took notice of Venetian Renaissance painting and like Prout he responded to the Venetian Gothic and to the Near Eastern atmosphere of the city. He may well have exaggerated the number of people wearing Turkish costume to be seen there in this period, and thus his paintings, although realistic and up to a point even impressionistic in style, are distinctly flavoured with Orientalist romanticism. The reality before him while he sketched was subtly transformed into the semi-fantasy in which the art dealers of Paris and London wanted to believe, for by now Bonington was beginning to be pursued by dealers. At the same time he was astute enough to take Canaletto's paintings as his starting point, at any rate in his finished pictures (both oil paintings and watercolours) executed after his return to Paris (plate 107), and the grouping of his figures is more like Canaletto's than is Turner's. He was quite without Turner's intellectual or classical interests and his work has little of Turner's breadth and mystery. Bonington was an *intimiste*; Turner an exponent of the sublime, even when working in watercolour and on a small scale. Significantly, Bonington's visit to Italy was confined to the northern part of the country – he never went to Rome – but he shared Turner's feeling for light. His oil sketches of Venice, which were presumably painted from nature and have no parallel in Turner's work, are unforgettably vivid.

A more dispiriting case is that of Clarkson Stanfield (1793–1867), who visited Venice for the first time in 1830 and exhibited his first Venetian oil painting at the Royal Academy the following year. Stanfield fell into the error of basing the handling and *chiaroscuro* of his Venetian paintings and watercolours (plate 109) on Turner's early seascapes – a decision which made them incongruously dull and heavy. It was rumoured at the time that his *Venice, from the Dogana* (fig. 7), shown at the Royal Academy in 1833, provoked Turner to paint 'in two or three days' his first Venetian oil picture, *Bridge of Sighs, Ducal Palace and Custom House, Venice: Canaletti painting* (plate 96), which appeared in the same exhibition. Both pictures were strongly influenced by Canaletto, and the composition of Stanfield's was also inspired by Prout's water-

7. Clarkson Stanfield, *Venice, from the Dogana*. R.A. 1833. Oil on canvas.
130 × 116.5 cm. The Earl of Shelburne

colour of 1826, an engraving of which was published in 1831. Contemporary critics, however, had no difficulty in perceiving the respective merits of the two works. One newspaper, *The Spectator*, said of the Stanfield, 'it is cleverly painted, but the unavoidable comparison with the same subject by Turner is fatal to it. It is to Turner's picture what a mere talent is to genius'. The Turner, on the other hand, was 'a most brilliant gem. The emerald waters, the bright blue sky, and the ruddy hue of the Ducal Palace, relieved by the chaste whiteness of the stone buildings around, combine to present a picture as bright, rich and harmonious in tone, as the actual scene painting can surpass the purity of colour. It is a perfectly beautiful picture'.[31] Yet it was Stanfield who received an offer for his *Venice, from the Dogana* and a commission for nine more pictures of Italian subjects from the Marquess of Lansdowne, and a further commission for five Venetian paintings from the Duchess of Sutherland. Turner, on the other hand, had to be content with the patronage of Robert Vernon, a humbly-born businessman who had made a fortune by supplying horses to the British Army during the Napoleonic Wars. Not that Vernon was a bad alternative; he was one of the two most active patrons of contemporary British artists, and in Turner's lifetime, in 1847, he gave his collection to the National Gallery, London.

It is in practice very unlikely that Turner's *Bridge of Sighs, Ducal Palace and Custom House, Venice: Canaletti painting*, one of the most elaborately executed of all his later works in oil despite its small size, was painted in rivalry with Clarkson Stanfield's picture included in the exhibition of 1833. If Turner was setting out to rival Stanfield, a more probable source of inspiration is the latter's *Diorama of Venice* shown at Drury Lane Theatre in December 1831.[32] Other developments also took place in the early 1830s that might have brought home to Turner the advantage of producing oil paintings of Venice. One was the posthumous popularity of Bonington, whom Turner admired.[33] Another was the fact that Venetian views were becoming common at the exhibitions of the Society of Painters in Water-Colours, although they remained surprisingly rare at the Royal Academy until the second half of the nineteenth century. At the

Academy, Turner continued to share the honours in 1834 and 1835 with Stanfield, the press again mistakenly assuming that the two artists were seeking to out-do each other; after that Turner had the field largely to himself. A further prompting in the direction of Venice, if Turner had needed one, could have been given by the commission for his finished watercolour of *The Ducal Palace* (plate 6), engraved as an illustration to the 1830 edition of Rogers's *Italy*, and by the Venetian view (plate 7) which was among the watercolours he executed in 1833 for Rogers's *Poems*.

If there was some element of opportunism in Turner's decision to add oil paintings of Venice to his repertoire this would not be out of character. He may well have been responding to the new climate of taste; and may also have felt that after the relative commercial and critical failure of his poetic paintings of classical subjects in the 1820s Venice would give him the means, in Hardy George's phrase, 'of expressing his poetic ideas in a more saleable manner'.[34] Whether or not these were his motives, he certainly succeeded in selling most of the Venetian pictures that he exhibited. What is more, the reviews of these pictures, with some notorious exceptions, were generally favourable. Nor would it have been out of character for Turner to have visited Venice after he had started painting pictures of the city: he had done just this in 1819. It is therefore appropriate to say something at this point about Turner's further visits to Venice. Then the watercolours of this period will be discussed; and finally we shall return to the oil paintings.

There is some uncertainty about the date of his second visit and, still more, about the dates of the watercolours and their manner of execution. Ever since A.J. Finberg's *Inventory . . . of the Turner Bequest* published in 1909, it has been known that the artist was in Venice in 1840.[35] In his book, *In Venice with Turner* (1930), Finberg gave further particulars of this visit, and, out of a number of possibilities vaguely implied in the *Inventory*, postulated a single intermediate visit in 1835, between those of 1819 and 1840. In his annotations to the British Museum copy of *In Venice with Turner*, C.F. Bell suggested that Turner had also been in Venice in 1832: he based this partly on what he saw as the

necessity of explaining the exhibited picture, *Bridge of Sighs . . . Canaletti painting*, of 1833, and partly on indications in some of Turner's pencil sketches of what he interpreted as scaffolding on the Campanile of St Mark's. He thought – wrongly – that this was in place in 1832 but not in 1835. More recently, and with better reason, Hardy George has rejected both these dates and has proposed that Turner visited Venice only once in the 1830s, in 1833.[36] The principal evidence for this is a reference in the *Gazzetta Privilegiata di Venezia* for 9 September of that year of 'Turner, gent. inglese' as arriving that day from Vienna. The probability that this 'Turner' was indeed the artist is lent weight by the sketchbook TB CCCXI, in which sketches of Vienna are followed by others of Linz, Salzburg, Innsbruck, Verona and finally Venice. There is no reference in the *Gazetta* to Turner's departure but according to his annotations in sketchbook TB CCCXII, which he himself marked 'from Venice up to Trento', he was in 'Botzen' (Bolzano) in the Dolomites on 22 September. He would thus have been in Venice for about ten days, during which time he would have made about 185 pencil sketches in three sketchbooks, TB CCCXI, CCCXIV (the most important, with about 175 sketches) and CCCXII.

There is nothing here that is inconsistent with what is otherwise known of Turner's activity, and Hardy George's suggestion that Turner paid his second visit to Venice in 1833 remains the most plausible hypothesis at present suggested. But it is not completely proven, in spite of some recent assertions. The possibility remains open that Turner may in addition have visited Venice in any one or more of the years 1835, 1837 and 1839, in each of which years there are references in his correspondence to his having been abroad for the summer months without any indication of where he went.[37] (As we have seen, the *Gazzetta*'s record of arrivals in and departures from the city was not infallible, and 'Turner' is a common English name which occurs at times when the artist could not have been meant; it is not out of the question that the Turner recorded as arriving on 9 September 1833 was someone else.) If the pencil sketches were all that had to be taken into account, there would be no need even to suppose that there had been more than one visit in the

1830s, but since there are over 150 Venetian watercolours in existence as well the possibility cannot be ruled out. This in turn raises the problem of whether all these watercolours were actually executed in Venice. The answer seems to be that some were and some were not: which returns us to the likelihood, but not the certainty, that Turner paid only two visits to Venice after 1819, one in 1833 and the other in 1840. Further light can be thrown on this problem only by the evidence contained in Turner's sketchbooks about all his later Continental journeys. This task will be carried out by Andrew Wilton in the course of his revision of the Finberg *Inventory*.

Fortunately, Turner's visit to Venice in 1840 is well documented. He left London, as was his usual habit, around the end of July and by about 10 August he had reached the Swiss-Austrian frontier at Bregenz. For at least part of the journey he had travelled with a certain 'E.H.' and his wife, who wrote to him later from Rome.[38] On 20 August, according to the *Gazzetta*, 'Turner S [sic]. M.W., gentilhuomo inglese'[39] arrived in Venice from Bolzano, a fact confirmed by sketches of that town and other places in the mountains between Bregenz and Belluno in his sketchbook, TB CCCXX. He left, also according to the *Gazzetta* ('Turner, J.M. inglese'), on 3 September for Trieste. By 17 September he was in Coburg in Central Germany making sketches (in TB CCCX) for his painting of *Schloss Rosenau*, the childhood home of Prince Albert, which appeared at the Royal Academy in 1841, and on 7 October he was back in London ('from Venice', as he wrote to a friend[40]). He was thus in Venice in 1840 for fourteen days, longer than on either previous visit. There can also be little doubt that this time Venice was the main objective of his journey. While there he made in all about 180 pencil sketches in three sketchbooks: TB CCCXX, CCCXIII (this contains the majority) and CCCX. A revealing glimpse of Turner during this visit occurs in the *Autobiography* of William Callow:

> The next time I met Turner was at Venice, at Hotel Europa, where we sat opposite at meals and entered into conversation. One evening whilst I was enjoying a cigar in a gondola I saw in another one Turner sketching San Giorgio, brilliantly lit up by the setting sun. I felt quite ashamed of myself idling away the time whilst he was hard at work so late.[41]

The pencil sketches executed in 1833 (which from now on will for convenience be assumed to be a definite date) and 1840 may be considered together. In the years that had elapsed since 1819 there had been some improvement in the city's economy.[42] Austrian rule had come to be even more bitterly resented by the middle classes. The first stirrings of the sentiment that was to lead to the revolution of 1848–9 could be felt, in spite of the fact that most taxes on goods entering and leaving Venice had been lifted. Gaslighting was introduced in the streets and steam vessels (see plate 89) appeared on the Lagoon. A bathing establishment was opened in 1833 at the entrance of the Grand Canal near the Punta della Dogana, though no sign of this is reflected in Turner's sketches and watercolours. Six theatres were open every evening during the summer, and Turner clearly attended on one or more occasions (plates 11, 19, 20). Tourism increased, and it has been estimated that in 1843, just before the completion of the causeway and the opening of the Milan-Venice railway in 1845, more than 100,000 visitors arrived in Venice, though the majority must surely have been Italians from the mainland with business there. Among the visitors from England in 1835 and 1841 were the Ruskin family, though the young John Ruskin did not realise that Turner, by 1841 already his hero, had recently preceded him on both occasions. To accommodate the influx of visitors, new hotels were opened, including the Europa in the former Palazzo Giustiniani opposite the Dogana at the entrance to the Grand Canal.

His pencil sketches dating from 1833 and 1840 (figs 8, 9) are more summary than those of 1819 and were executed with a blunter point. They can hardly have been used for reference purposes. Instead they were perhaps a form of mental exercise, a means of registering the process of observation; as he looked at a motif and took in its essential shape and character, so the impression which formed itself in his brain was jotted down. All this would have gone on at high speed. Sometimes the process would have been comparatively mechanical, as he re-drew subjects, especially around the entrance to the Grand Canal and across the water from the Europa to S. Giorgio Maggiore and S. Maria della Salute, that he had studied in detail in 1819. At other times he was sketching new subjects, including such architectural details as arches and parts of buildings, narrow alleyways and side-canals. It is evident, in short, that although Turner may have executed his pencil sketches more rapidly than before, he gave himself more time to penetrate the interior of the city and even to go into St Mark's (plates 14, 15). Nevertheless, he continued to ignore Venetian painting. Although he produced a brilliant watercolour of the exterior of *The Accademia* (plate 91), he appears never to have gone inside. As in 1819, the endlessly fascinating relationships of buildings, water and sky, seen under a variety of atmospheric conditions, absorbed his imagination to the exclusion of almost everything else.

Now to consider the watercolours. They are mostly grouped in five sections of the Turner Bequest, CCCXV–CCCXIX, with several more in the 'Miscellaneous' section, CCCXLIV; some from this section are no more than 'colour beginnings', that is, sheets with colour washes on them but without any definite indications of form. In addition, at least twenty-six Venetian watercolours by Turner are outside the Bequest.[43] The grand total is about 170. The handling varies from very summary and almost crude to quite elaborate and extremely refined, though no watercolour is a finished work of art as the artist and his patrons understood the term. It is possible that Turner hoped to obtain commissions for finished versions of some of his watercolour sketches, as he was to do in the case of those executed in Switzerland in the early 1840s. However, nothing came of this with the material he brought back from Venice. All that happened was that two dozen of the more finished sheets were bought by patrons, probably through the artist's dealer, Thomas Griffith.[44] Two-thirds of these, including at least five and probably all six bought by Ruskin,[45] once formed part of the group listed as CCCXV in the Turner Bequest.

8. (*above*) J.M.W. Turner, *The Grand Canal, looking towards the Dogana and S. Giorgio Maggiore*. 1833. Pencil 111 × 203 mm (TB CCCXIV-80)

9. (*below*) J.M.W. Turner, *Looking towards SS. Giovanni e Paolo*. 1833. Pencil. 109 × 203 mm (TB CCCXIV-56)

The watercolours in the Bequest vary considerably in size, type of paper and style. CCCXVIII–IX (see plates 8–29) are all on brown paper, measuring on average either 230 × 300 mm or 150 × 230 mm. The sheets on which these are executed were probably cut freehand by Turner with scissors from larger pieces of paper, the smaller size being produced by cutting the 'standard' size in half. The handling of this group of watercolours is very broad, like that of the pencil sketches from the 1833 and 1840 visits, though some are of extraordinary aesthetic quality. The colours are mainly red and blue with shades of both dark and light brown; white heightening is added. Where the blue is applied thinly it is toned down by the brown paper underneath. The red, however, always stands out. As in the distant view of Venice of 1819 (plate 4), red tends to come forward, blue to lie back; the colours thus play a part in the creation of the pictorial space. Moreover, through its effect on the tones and colours, this brown paper influences the choice of subject-matter and the time of day represented. Wide vistas and bright light become more difficult to render, and many of these watercolours therefore show close-up views, such as street scenes, small bridges, prospects glimpsed through arches, and the interiors of theatres and shops. In one (plate 25), Turner depicts the Porta della Carta in some detail, a composition consisting entirely of Byzantine and Gothic buildings which are rendered with a sure understanding of their structure; of all Turner's Venetian watercolours this is the one that most nearly anticipates Ruskin's treatment of such subjects at the time he was working on *The Stones of Venice*. (It is curious at first sight that Turner should have been so reluctant to become closely engaged with Venetian medieval architecture, given that he had been a superb draughtsman of English Gothic cathedrals and abbeys in his youth; however, English artists and critics found the Gothic of their own country acceptable long before they took its Italian equivalents seriously.)

Another consequence of the use of brown paper is that the majority of these watercolours are night scenes. The beauty of Venice by night was already beginning to be appreciated by travellers, and this is magically evoked in, for example, *St Mark's from the Piazzetta* (plate 8) where the mixture of white and blue used for the domes of the cathedral creates the effect of moonlight. Finer still, perhaps, is the last of the group illustrated here, *S. Maria della Salute: night scene with rockets* (plate 29). This is a more complete composition than the others and shows the church from the familiar viewpoint on the opposite side of the Grand Canal, from the steps of the Hotel Europa. The recession of space at the left between the dark mass of the Dogana, defined by its three lighted windows, and the dimly perceived outlines of the boats is brilliantly characteristic of Turner's art. No earlier painter had expressed so simply yet so skilfully the dark, luminous surface of calm water at night.

Where and when were these watercolours executed? No answers to this question can by anything but tentative. The consistency of style and treatment and of the manner in which the paper is cut suggests that they all belong to a single period of time. One clue to their dating is surely hard to resist: three of them (plates 12, 13, 28) show a view of roof-tops looking east towards the Campanile of St Mark's. This is the underlying compositional theme of the oil painting, *Juliet and her Nurse* (plate 97), exhibited in 1836. In addition, one of these watercolours (plate 28) includes fireworks bursting over the Canale di San Marco, a motif which also occurs in the picture. Might Turner have executed all three one evening from his bedroom at the top of the Hotel Europa? It is not impossible. At all events, a visual experience of this sort seems to underlie both the watercolours and the oil painting, although in the latter the viewpoint is shifted some distance to the left so as to take in the Piazza of St Mark's (no corresponding view occurs among the pencil sketches). If this is correct, it would be an argument for dating all the watercolours on brown paper to Turner's second visit to Venice, which is here assumed to have taken place in 1833, though a 'postponement' of that visit to 1835 would fit the pictorial evidence better. (Another reason for preferring 1835 is that there appears to be a more than coincidental resemblance between plate 27, showing the canal beneath the Bridge of Sighs, and Etty's oil painting of the same subject, fig. 5, exhibited in the spring of that year at the Royal Academy.) 1833 (or 1835), rather than 1840, is also suggested for these watercolours by their similarity to another group executed by Turner on blue paper in the late 1820s at Petworth.

It does not follow that all, or even any, of Turner's Venetian watercolours on brown paper were executed from nature. Those showing scenes in theatres or outdoors at night almost certainly were not. Even the views of the Campanile seen across the roof-tops may have been done from memory; all that seems certain is that they, and the related motif in *Juliet and her Nurse*, are not imaginary. Conversely, it is likely on *a priori* grounds that some of this group *were* done out of doors; the *Porta della Carta* is perhaps the most obvious example. As we have seen when discussing the results of the 1819 tour, there is no clear stylistic distinction in Turner's work between watercolours executed from nature and those executed in his hotel room, at some point later in his tour, or even back in London (we are speaking here, of course, of watercolour sketches; finished watercolours were almost invariably executed in London or in houses where Turner had the use of a studio, such as Farnley Hall and Petworth). The handling and lack of detail of the Venetian watercolours on brown paper suggests that they were executed very rapidly, with perhaps several being worked on simultaneously. Even bearing in mind the number of pencil sketches Turner made during the ten days he was in Venice in 1833, he could have produced all forty of these watercolours as well. But not necessarily; they could have been executed later. Improbable though it seems, even the 1840 visit cannot totally be ruled out.

Another group of watercolours that may conceivably be associated with Turner's second visit to Venice is listed among TB CCCXVI – listed 'among' rather than 'as' because this section of the Turner Bequest, also entitled by Finberg 'Venice: Miscellaneous', contains sheets of various sizes. About twenty-eight of them, however, are the same size (approximately 243 × 305 mm) and had clearly once formed the leaves of a sketchbook. Eighteen are illustrated here.[46] Directly they are extracted from the rest they can be seen to be consistent with one another in style, for the most part rather pale in tone,

impressionistic in character and with the detail only sketchily indicated. The paper throughout is off-white.

The reasons for thinking that this group might date from 1833 are, first, that several sheets are watermarked 1828 and, second, that one of them (plate 74) depicts a view across roof-tops towards the Campanile of St Mark's comparable to those on brown paper just discussed, except that the scene is here shown in daylight. Because of the use of white paper and transparent watercolour, this group introduces us for the first time to the mysterious dream world that Turner conjured up in all his later representations of Venice, whether in watercolour on paper or oil on canvas. To distinguish sharply between this group and others of the late period would be capricious. In all of them, solid forms blend into the surrounding water and sky, objects are hardly more substantial than their reflections, and time seems suspended. These effects are created largely by floating a second, stronger wash of colour on to a first while the first is still wet and by detaching the details from the forms of which they are in reality a part. The result is that the representation looks like an image projected in coloured lights on to a gauze screen rather than an illusionary recreation of reality on an impermeable surface. In a few cases, notably plates 58, 61 and 84, Turner began with a pencil outline, probably sketched from nature, but the first application of colour was in broad, dilute washes of grey, yellow or blue, after which more concentrated washes of yellow, blue, green and occasionally red were run into them. As the colour began to dry he added crisper accents to give definition to the buildings, boats and figures, and in a number of instances finished off the watercolour with lines drawn with a pen in red ink. These lines do not so much reinforce the wash as lie on top of it, or, visually, hover in front of the forms which the wash represents. A kind of brightly coloured irregular grid appears superimposed on the composition, giving it movement and vitality.

Sometimes – see especially plates 63 and 64 – an impression is conveyed of the amazing quantity of imagery that assaults the eye from certain viewpoints in Venice, like an enormous kaleidoscope. At other times, for example in plates 52, 58 and 84, the composition contains only a few comparatively simple forms looming faintly out of the mist or heat haze. Almost always, however, the view is an open one with water as its foreground feature. Favourite subjects are the Piazzetta and Ducal Palace seen from the Giudecca or S. Giorgio Maggiore, the entrance to the Grand Canal from a point near the Accademia, and the line of the Riva degli Schiavoni with the Ducal Palace and Campanile viewed from the mouth of the Rio dell'Arsenale. When depicting the latter, Turner shows his capacity to create a sharply receding vista leading the eye along a line of light which exaggerates the distance between the eye and the object furthest from it. In all of these watercolours the pictorial space is filled with light, though a light diffused by mist or filtered through a thin layer of cloud. In several, we gaze into the setting sun, or the sun casts a yellow or orange glow over distant buildings.

In two, however, the colour is much stronger than in the others. In the drawing of *The Arsenal* (plate 75), the only close-up view in the group, in which it is far from clear how the buildings as shown correspond to those in reality, Turner has given the composition an unreal, fiery red colour-scheme. It is true that, as Ruskin observed, even the trees in the public gardens of Venice often appear bright red in the light of the setting sun, as if they were on fire,[47] but in the watercolour of *The Arsenal* Turner does not seem to show the light coming from any particular direction. It is as if he had started from the fact of the red brick, which then transformed itself in his imagination into the walls of a furnace symbolising the great armaments factory which the Arsenal had once been. No stranger as an artist to industrial subject matter, he depicts the building as a massive fortress, behind the far wall of which the masts of tall ships can be seen but whose foreground is almost empty of figures.

The other strongly coloured watercolour in this group (plate 83) is also without figures and, indeed, almost without buildings. Identified as Venice chiefly by the line of posts used to mark a channel in the Lagoon, it depicts one of those flaming Venetian sunsets which writers from Aretino onwards had enthusiastically described but which, until Turner, no artist since the Renaissance had painted – and even Renaissance artists used sunsets only as backgrounds to figure compositions. Turner's watercolour is the first to make a sunset over the Lagoon the subject of an entire picture. The clouds at the top are coloured crimson and purple, the latter colour being echoed dimly in a line drawn with the brush to mark the horizon. The main part of the sky is yellow and, below that, the mist over the horizon is orange-red. The water is bluish green, made up of three different tones of the same colour. Thanks to the omission of descriptive detail, the gondola in the centre and the coarse grasses growing from a submerged mud-flat at the right lose their distinctness and partake of the enchanted nature of the scene. The colours chosen may be a subconscious illustration of Turner's understanding of colour science as expounded (not very clearly) in his Royal Academy lectures on perspective. All the positive colours are 'aerial' or light colours, not the local colours of objects. Darkness, he thought, was 'the privation of colour' and was obtained by mixing all the others. It appears here in the mud-colour used for the posts, the gondola and the grasses.[48] It almost goes without saying that none of this group of watercolours is likely to have been more than minimally coloured on the spot. They may not even have been executed in Venice.

The next group, also consisting of about twenty-seven sheets, of which thirteen are illustrated here (plates 30–42), is listed as TB CCCXVII. These are on light grey paper measuring on average 192 × 280 mm. It is not clear whether the sheets were originally loose or constituted a sketchbook. It is certain, however, that they date from Turner's final visit to Venice because one of them (plate 30) shows the Campanile of St Mark's with scaffolding around its pinnacle, and this structure was only in place in 1840. It is inconceivable that Turner would have included it if it had not been there, though he often leaves it out, especially in distant views – something that he would have been all the more likely to do in watercolours not executed from nature. There is one other sheet, on off-white paper, plate 56, in which the scaffolding is conspicuously evident, and the inscription on the *verso*, 'From my Bedroom, Venice', tends to confirm that it was drawn and coloured from the motif. The watercolours on grey paper, like those on brown, are frequently heightened with white, and they also include a number of close-up views such as the Palazzo Tasca-Papafava (plates 39, 40). They are in some ways the most decorative of all Turner's Venetian watercolours, with a predominance of blue, white and yellow. The grey paper did not lend itself to the use of blended colour washes and, more than elsewhere, Turner here plays around with semi-isolated patches of pure colour: blue for parts of the sky, yellow for a sail, green here and there for the water, and white for the highlights on buildings. Sometimes red pen-lines are used to accentuate details, as in the group of watercolours on off-white paper described above. Slight pencil under-drawing, possibly executed from nature, is common, and the whole series has an almost Bonington-like crispness and airiness, very unlike the watercolours on brown paper. The view of *S. Giorgio Maggiore* (plate 78) is the same size and may once have been part of this series, although it is on off-white paper. The flat washes of blue, buff and brick-red are here applied to forms arranged parallel to the picture surface and conform to a pattern of verticals, joining the form to its reflection, in a way reminiscent of the watercolours of Cézanne.

The most perfect, inventive and dream-like of Turner's watercolours of Venice are those listed as TB CCCXV, to which, as has already been mentioned, the majority of those bought by private collectors also belong. The sheets, which are of off-white paper measuring on average 222 × 322 mm, once formed part of a soft-backed sketchbook, called by Finberg a 'roll sketchbook' because the artist could roll it up in his pocket, though of all Turner's sketchbooks it is perhaps the one least likely to have been used in this way. Thirteen of the watercolours still in the Bequest are illustrated here, plates 43–55, and a further nine from those in other collections. Several sheets are watermarked 1834 which proves, if Turner's second visit to Venice occurred in 1833, that they must either have been executed in the years after his return from the city in 1833 or more probably after his visit of 1840. They would almost certainly be associated with this period in any case, partly for stylistic reasons and partly because the dealer, Griffith, would no doubt have offered patrons examples of the artist's most recent work.

Some of this group, such as plates 43–45, have the simple, impressionistic clarity of the series on grey paper. Plate 43, with its washes of pure blue for the sky, pale yellowish-pink for the buildings and blue-green brushed on in vertical strokes for the water even recalls the view of *The Campanile and Ducal Palace* (plate 5) of 1819. Others in the series, including plate 44, take up the motif of the Rialto Bridge which had been one of Turner's obsessions in that year. In general, however, this group is more complex both in its use of blended colours and in the relationships it establishes with reality than any that Turner had produced before. The ordinary words 'red', 'blue', 'green', etc. no longer seem appropriate, and because of the transparency and brilliance (not intensity) of the colours it is tempting to invoke the analogy of precious and semi-precious stones: emerald, turquoise, sapphire, amethyst, topaz, garnet, and so on. Turner takes advantage of a special property of watercolour here. By diluting the colour with water and thus allowing the white of the paper to show through, the colour keeps its brilliance while losing some of its natural depth of tone. The effect, if only to a limited degree, is literally that obtained by placing a coloured filter in front of a light source; and since, as we have seen, it was light colour rather than local colour that he wanted to represent, this effect was exactly what he needed. It is very noticeable that, in his late Venetian watercolours, the colours of the sky and the water are almost invariably stronger than those of the buildings (*The Arsenal*, already discussed, is an exception, as is the view of *The Accademia*, plate 91).

The colouring of these watercolours is not only transparent and brilliant; it is also, of course, unnatural. Turner did not reproduce a familiar reality but created a new one. The Venetian sky, water and architecture are magical enough in themselves. Turner produced not a superior version of this, as classical aesthetics would have had it, but a different truth, more strange and visionary. The areas of colour are often extraordinary in shape and conflict with the characteristic outlines of Venice. At times in these last watercolours, it seems to have been not so much the buildings that interested Turner but the boats (plates 44–48), and those are flicked in with a few curving strokes of the brush so that they appear to float on top of the water like wicker baskets, hardly breaking its surface. It is in fact not easy to 'see' Turner's Venice in the real city, except perhaps from a distance. He hints at the decay of parts of modern Venice and at the harshness of modern life, while at the same time conjuring up a vision of the past; not the past at any particular moment in time (he reveals no nostalgia for the *ancien régime*) but a city in a state of 'becoming' rather than 'being'. In Byron's words:

> I saw from out the wave her structures rise
> As from the stroke of the enchanter's wand.

It is no coincidence that several of the watercolours are not easy to explain topographically; they are, in short, inventions. And while there is no doubt that Turner sketched a good deal from nature during his last visit, sometimes in colour – we have William Callow's testimony for this, besides inherent probability – the possibility arises that he continued to paint watercolours of Venice after his return to London. This is supported by the resemblance between some of those in TB CCCXV and the oil paintings of the period, 1842–6: compare, for example, plates 49, 50, 51, 69 and 102–5. In both groups, the elegant vertical forms of domes and towers which had previously dominated Turner's compositions tend to fade into insignificance or be excluded altogether, to be replaced by an unbroken line or lines of low buildings. One characteristic background is formed by the Riva degli Schiavoni filling the picture from side to side, as in the watercolour, plate 69, and the oil painting, *The Sun of Venice going to Sea* (plate 103). An alternative scheme is for converging lines of buildings to frame a deep vista, with gondolas pointing the way towards it (plate 51 and *San Benedetto looking towards Fusina*, 1843, fig. 10). In both types, the execution is by countless fine, mostly vertical lines placed close together, either in red ink using a pen or in watercolour applied with a brush (watercolour seems to be used for this purpose even in the oil paintings). The more nearly finished Turner's watercolours are, the more the execution depends on fine strokes placed side by side and overlapping, rather than on broadly applied washes.

Turner's last group of watercolours also includes four storm scenes (plates 86–9), all of which, interestingly enough, were acquired by patrons – perhaps they found them easier to understand than the artist's highly coloured, very personal watercolours of Venice in calm weather. Storms on the Lagoon were by then being described in Romantic travel literature, and Turner experienced at least one storm in 1840 (he also saw lightning behind the Campanile of St Mark's one night in 1833, to judge from plate 12). Because of the shallowness of the water the wind does no more than agitate the surface, and the drama is concentrated in the sky. From long experience, Turner had learnt how to express the movement of the clouds directly by the movement of his brush. A few upward sweeps of the brush in grey, blue or reddish-brown – partly floated into, partly dragged over, the paler wash underneath – are enough, while some lighter areas are obtained by wiping or sponging out parts of the colour.

The watercolour that may serve to sum up this group is the view of *The Accademia* (plate 91), once owned by Ruskin and now in the Ashmolean Museum. Ethereal, calm and abstracted, the dream of a water-borne world, it perfectly combines both suggestiveness and completeness. Neither in composition nor in colour is it conventionally beautiful. The shapes of the buildings are unyieldingly rectangular, the reliance on primary colours inevitably produces a slightly discordant effect, and the penwork used to describe architectural detail is almost scratchy. But these qualities are evidence of Turner's boldness and his refusal to succumb to the allure of the merely pretty. What gives the work its irresistible appeal is the treatment of the light. Turner has chosen, or imagined, a misty late afternoon. The sun is almost in line with the canal façade of the Accademia (the former church of the Carità), so that oblique shadows are cast by the Gothic cornice on to the otherwise illuminated wall. Both sunlit and shadowed parts of the composition are, however, softened by the mist, as is also true of the reflections in the water. These reflections are hardly more than abstract patches of colour; the sharply defined architectural forms trail downwards without interruption into the water, to become lost in shimmering indistinctness.

Ruskin described this and two other watercolours from the

10. J.M.W. Turner, *St Benedetto, looking towards Fusina*. R.A. 1843. Oil on canvas. 61.5 × 92 cm. The Tate Gallery, London (534). B/J 406

series when he gave them to the Ashmolean Museum in 1861 as 'sketches on the spot':[49] a surprising judgement, it may be thought, in view of all that has been said here about this series. Was Ruskin right? The shadows on the façade of the Accademia are so precisely observed as to give one pause before contradicting him out of hand. And yet, while it is easy to imagine some watercolours being executed from nature and others in the artist's hotel room, it is harder to believe that the sketchbook was begun in Venice and continued later in London. The watercolours exhibit great variety, but it is the variety typical of a spectrum, not that of two distinct categories. Is it conceivable that in addition to doing a good deal of sketching out of doors in pencil, Turner executed over 60 mostly quite complex watercolours (if those on grey paper are included) during his final visit to Venice, even though he was there for what was for him the comparatively long period of fourteen days? This is a question which for the time being seems insoluble. But it is one of more than academic interest, for if we knew the answer we should have a better understanding of Turner's creative procedure.

As we have seen, Turner's first two oil paintings of Venice – *Bridge of Sighs, Ducal Palace and Custom House, Venice: Canaletti painting* (Tate Gallery; plate 96) and the lost, Bonington-like *Ducal Palace, Venice* – were exhibited in 1833, before his second visit. The view shown in the former, from the Isola di S. Giorgio Maggiore, had occurred several times in his sketchbooks of 1819. If he had needed further information about the architecture, he could easily have turned to paintings by, or engravings after, Canaletto, as did Clarkson Stansfield for his picture also exhibited in 1833 (fig. 7). Nevertheless, there are some architectural peculiarities in Turner's painting. First, and most obviously, the wall of the Dogana has been slewed round through almost ninety degrees; it should in fact be almost parallel to the line of the Ducal Palace and the prominent Renaissance building to the left of it, the Mint (for the oddity of 'Canaletti painting' in the open air, see the note on the plate). Second, there are mistakes in the painting of the Ducal Palace; neither in this picture nor in others did Turner grasp the visual

significance of the two dropped windows at the right-hand, or eastern, end of the façade – a fault for which Ruskin unfairly chided Canaletto, who usually got this detail right. Turner also employs artist's licence to 'unblock' the five righthand bays of the lower arcade, which were bricked up at this date to support the façade above them.

In one respect, however, Turner showed that he understood both the scene itself and the paintings of Canaletto better than either Stanfield or Prout. This is in his treatment of space. In his painting, unlike theirs, the expanse of the Bacino di San Marco is given both breadth and depth, and its surface is alive with interest, not only with boats but also with a range of colours in the water. The eye is carried across the dark foreground to the panorama of buildings on the far side and even, as it were, round the Punta della Dogana almost to the entrance of the Grand Canal. Another memorable feature of this painting is the use of white highlights to render the bleached appearance of the stone; the buildings seen all along their edges to be encrusted with icing sugar – a feat which the artist's watercolours were less capable of achieving. Both this and the colours used for the buildings are unusually realistic in the context of Turner's Venetian works. Brick is rendered as brick-red, the facing tiles of the Ducal Palace as rose-pink, the marble and unbleached stones in a neutral grey. The sky, where not covered by a few thin clouds, is a conventional deep blue. In its realistic colours, strong tone contrasts, tight organisation and careful finish, this is, in short, as might be expected, the most 'Old Master-ish' of Turner's Venetian pictures: which is not to say that anyone but he could have painted it or that the exotic fabrics piled up in the boats at the left were not a pictorial invention peculiarly his own.

From 1833 to 1846, Turner exhibited at least one Venetian painting at the Royal Academy every year except 1838 and 1839. As already mentioned, they were for the most part well received by the critics and the majority were sold. The buyers were nearly all collectors belonging to the new industrialist and merchant class, men such as Henry McConnell (textile manufacturer), Robert Vernon (horse-dealer), John Sheepshanks (cloth manufacturer), Elhanan Bicknell (whaling entrepreneur), Edwin

11. William Miller after J.M.W. Turner, *Venice from the Porch of Madonna della Salute*. Engraving (R.648). 1838. 375 × 582 mm

Bullock (iron-master) and B.G. Windus (coachmaker). Even Ruskin, the son of a sherry merchant, was by origin from this class, though the one Venetian painting by Turner that he owned – *The Grand Canal* (fig. 12), now in the Huntington Art Gallery – was not bought until ten years after it was exhibited (in 1837). The only 'aristocratic' patron that Turner had for his Venetian pictures was the Scottish landowner, H.A.J. Munro of Novar. The popularity of these pictures is further attested by the fact that very few remained unfinished; plate 98 is one of them.

In 1834 Turner exhibited *Venice* (National Gallery of Art, Washington) and in 1835 *Venice, from the Porch of Madonna della Salute* (Metropolitan Museum, New York; for engraving see fig. 11).[50] Both show the entrance to the Grand Canal looking eastwards with the Dogana on the right, the former being taken from a viewpoint on the Canal to the left of and just beyond the boat with banners displayed aloft, in the latter. Both compositions are more open and lighter in tone than *Bridge of Sighs . . . Canaletti painting*; in fact, in the Metropolitan picture, Turner exaggerates the width of the Grand Canal in the foreground and wrongly makes it seem to become narrower towards its entrance. What is more, both paintings appear to depend on drawings made in 1819 and both have the stillness and descriptive clarity associated with his artistic approach to Venice during that period, though they are not necessarily incompatible in feeling with watercolours from the section, TB CCCXVI, which date from his second or third visit.

However this may be, there is no doubt that *Juliet and her Nurse* (plate 97) of 1836 marked a new creative departure. With this we are introduced to a far more profound and poetic vision than Turner had yet conjured up. It is surely the most evocative Venetian picture he ever painted. And by a fortunate co-incidence, it found a literary response worthy of it, for it was the occasion of the début of the young Ruskin as a critic of painting. This took the form of his famous *Reply* (never published at the time) to the attack in *Blackwood's Magazine* on Turner's three pictures exhibited at the Academy in 1836, of which *Juliet and her Nurse* was one. Although he defended the naturalistic basis of the painting, Ruskin grasped at once that a world beyond and above that of ordinary everyday experience was being evoked:

> Many-coloured mists are floating above the distant City, but such mists as you might imagine to be aetherial spirits, souls of the mighty dead breathed out of the tombs of Italy into the blue of her bright heaven, and wandering in vague and infinite glory around the earth that they have loved.

(For further extracts from Ruskin's *Reply*, see the note to plate 97.) Both figures and setting partake of this dream world. It is of no serious account that neither Juliet nor her nurse ever set foot in Venice – perhaps Turner simply hit upon this Shakespeare play rather than another one by accident. In any case, there is a further anachronism in the figures in the Piazza, who are all dressed like people from a painting by Watteau. Did Turner look out of his bedroom window in the Hotel Europa one night and find the crowd below transformed in his imagination into a fancy-dress ball – the Capulets' ball? And did 'Juliet and her nurse' (the two figures on the balcony at the bottom right) spring from that hallucination? What is extraordinary is that the greatest precision is lavished on those details of the setting which are most peripheral: the chimney-pots, the façades of the buildings lining the square (the Procuratie Vecchie and the Procuratie Nuove), the clock-tower, the gondola-lined sweep of the Riva degli Schiavoni, the Mint (moved about 50 yards eastwards from its true position). In the distance on the right, next to S. Giorgio Maggiore, Turner imagines a new structure erected in the Bacino di San Marco, or perhaps another small island, from which fireworks soar into the night. The climax to the setting – St Mark's, the Ducal Palace and the Campanile, towards which everything is directed – seem by comparison a gathering of spectres. St Mark's is like an unfinished model for part of a stage set. The Ducal Palace to its right is hardly more substantial. In front of St Mark's, to the left of centre in the composition and balancing the figures at the bottom right, the Campanile stands paper-thin, as if it hardly had the strength to support its own weight. With its pale and ghostly forms, its hushed atmosphere and soft blue and gold colour scheme, *Juliet and her Nurse* is the most elegiac and reticent of Turner's

Venetian paintings. It is actually less flamboyant though not less spellbinding than Ruskin's description of it suggests, and is certainly less strident than the next Venetian picture Turner painted, *The Grand Canal, Venice* (1837) in the Huntington Art Gallery (fig. 12),[51] which also had a Shakespearian theme.

When Turner came back to the Academy with two Venetian subjects in 1840 (plates 99, 100), he chose strong sunlight and predominantly warm colour schemes. The buildings are either pale yellow or white, and a good deal of red appears among the figures and boats. As in *Bridge of Sighs . . . Canaletti painting*, the Bacino di San Marco occupies the foreground, and boats laden with exotic goods float in clusters on its surface. However, the forms are softer-edged now and blend more into each other, while at the same time the reflections spread deeper into the water like stains spreading through damp cloth. In both pictures, Turner paints a more 'populist' Venice than before, with traders and their wares assuming dominant roles in the composition. The Venetian history he points to in *Venice, the Bridge of Sighs* (plate 99) is the ambiguous one evoked in the opening two lines of *Childe Harold's Pilgrimage*, which he used in the Royal Academy catalogue to accompany the picture, and which he misquoted:

> I stood upon a bridge, a palace and
> A prison on each hand. – *Byron.*

Following his return from his last visit to Venice in 1840, Turner's compositions became more extended and the buildings were now situated further back in space. *The Dogano, San Giorgio, Citella from the Steps of the Europa* (plate 101; 'Citella' is the church of Le Zitelle visible to the left of the Dogana), exhibited in 1842, is based on two watercolours from 1819 (plates 2, 3) placed side by side; but the differences are as instructive as the similarities. By exaggerating the disparity in scale between

12. J.M.W. Turner, *The Grand Canal, Venice*. R.A. 1837. Oil on canvas. 148 × 110.5 cm. Henry E. Huntington Library and Art Gallery, San Marino, California. B/J 368

the Dogana and the two churches in the background, Turner has increased the apparent distance between them and hence the depth of the composition. As if to compensate, he has given S. Giorgio an imposing palace or monastic building on either side of it, only the right-hand one of which is there, much smaller, in reality. This picture is more thinly painted than his other Venetian works in oil, and the hues and tones of the water have all the variety and delicacy of the washes used in his late watercolours. Unlike *The Campo Santo, Venice* in the same exhibition, however, the painting is not a great inventive masterpiece.

For *The Campo Santo*, Ruskin once more rose to the occasion, this time in volume I of *Modern Painters* (1843). It is true that the relevant passage, which is re-printed here on p. 80, refers to more than just this picture; it is a kind of composite evocation of all Turner's paintings of Venice, which is perhaps why Ruskin suppressed it in subsequent editions of the book, on the grounds of its being a literary deception. However, the passage contains at least two sentences which can only have been inspired by *The Campo Santo*: 'Do we dream, or does the white forked sail drift nearer, and nearer yet . . . It pauses now; but the quivering of its bright reflection troubles the shadows of the sea, those azure, fathomless depths of crystal mystery . . .'. Boats with twin sails had appeared in Turner's last Venetian watercolours but, apart from *The Sun of Venice going to Sea*, this is the only oil painting in which one is prominent. Juxtaposed with the (new) cemetery, the white sails seem like an angel's wings, or the soul of a dead person come to haunt the Lagoon. This is without doubt the most beautiful of Turner's Lagoon paintings. The warm blue used for the sky, the water and the distant hills is as expressive in its way as the colder blue of *Juliet and her Nurse*. There the mood was elegiac. Here it is peaceful and serene.

The co-existence of life and death is more explicitly the theme of *The Sun of Venice going to Sea* (plate 103), exhibited in 1843. Death, principally death by water, was the theme of three other paintings by him at the Royal Academy that year: *The Opening of the Walhalla*, *The Evening of the Deluge* and *The Morning after the Deluge*.[52] For all four he composed a despairing 'quotation'

from his MS poem, *Fallacies of Hope*. That for *The Sun of Venice* reads:

> Fair shines the morn, and soft the zephyrs blow,
> Venezia's fisher spreads his painted sail so gay
> Nor heeds the demon that in grim repose
> Expects his evening prey.

The superficial meaning of this is straightforward: the boat sails proudly out to sea, its crew unaware that they will be drowned by evening. But it is hard to resist the conclusion that it is Venice that is doomed, Venice that had enjoyed so glorious and colourful a history, which was now coming to an end.

It is part of the point, of course, that the picture is very attractive. Fishing-boats with red and yellow painted sails are the subject of one of Turner's most delightful late Venetian watercolours (plate 95), and for the view of the city he may have made use of another watercolour, *The Riva degli Schiavoni from the channel to the Lido* (plate 64), though this is one of those that were perhaps executed in 1833 rather than 1840. Both this watercolour and the painting are topographically inexact, for the long section of waterfront from west of the Piazzetta almost to the Public Gardens cannot be seen at this angle from so far away; rather than appear out to the left, as it does in the painting, S. Giorgio Maggiore would block the view in the centre. However, this is essentially a quibble. The beautifully painted city, white with countless fine vertical strokes of pink, pale blue and yellow laid on top in watercolour, serves as a more than adequate foil to the fishing-boats and the lightly disturbed sea depicted in the foreground. Ruskin greatly admired the manner in which the sea was painted and regarded it as an object lesson in the management of recession without the aid of 'objects all over [the surface] to tell the story by perspective'.

The Sun of Venice going to Sea was Ruskin's favourite among Turner's Venetian pictures (not that he bothered with its pessimistic 'message'), and it was, surely, the last in which the artist showed himself at the height of his powers. Nevertheless, there was a total of nine more exhibited and at least four unfinished pictures of Venetian subjects still to come between

1844 and 1846. The treatment of form in these is increasingly hazy. Hardly anything is described any more; it is only suggested or evoked. Buildings tend to look like rough-textured sea-shells and boats like blobs of reddened fur or upturned baskets. Architecture is now less important than before and boats more so. Turner was more concerned than ever with the idea of slow movement: the 'approach' to Venice, 'going to' and 'coming from' the ball. The predominant motif of his late Venetian pictures is a procession of boats, of boats drifting as if carried along by a slow current, not propelled by man. In 1845, he used Venice to illustrate the four times of day, although, as contemporary critics noted, he made little attempt to distinguish between them through differences of tone. As the titles of two of the pictures, *Venice, Evening, going to the Ball* (plate 104) and *Morning, returning from the Ball, St. Martino* (both of which he painted twice) indicate, he was still fascinated by Venice's past reputation as a festive city.

Unfortunately, it is not easy to appreciate Turner's late Venetian oil paintings today, as their condition is in most cases so unsatisfactory. What to us seem rectangles of cracked dirty yellow paint, incorporating the pale forms of buildings and the darker forms of boats, perceived as if in a fog, were to at least some contemporaries dazzling arrangements of colour. As the critic of *The Spectator* writing about *The Approach to Venice*, exhibited in 1844, said: 'beautiful as it is in colour it is but a vision of enchantment'.[53]

For some twenty years before and after Turner's death in 1851, the only artist to attempt to imitate his late style was J.B. Pyne (1800–1870). In 1835 he began travelling on the Continent and in the 1850s and 1860s produced several views of Venice (fig. 13) in the manner of Turner's first oil paintings of the city, though with hardly any of Turner's grandeur or poetry. During this period it was Bonington who was the principal influence. From the mid-1830s onwards, his followers, including James Holland (1799–1870), William Callow (1812–1908), David Roberts (1796–1864) and William Wyld (1806–1889), made successful careers out of exhibiting and selling Venetian views, among other subjects, in watercolours. Ruskin, as we have seen,

13. James Baker Pyne, *S. Giorgio Maggiore from the Dogana*. 1859. Oil on canvas. 48 × 64 cm. Private Collection

14. Albert Goodwin, *Venetian lagoons*. 1911. Watercolour with bodycolour.
280 × 375 mm. Private Collection

learnt his style of drawing Venetian architecture from Prout, as did W.J. Müller (1812–1845), who is one of the first artists known to have stayed at the Hotel Europa, in the autumn of 1834. In 1850, the marine painter E.W. Cooke, whose father and uncle were two of Turner's engravers, visited Venice for the first time and began painting views of the city in oils, using a style based on Turner's early seascapes. Edward Pritchett (*fl.*1828–64) and his follower Alfred Pollentine (*fl.*1861–80) were tireless *pasticheurs* of Canaletto. Henry Pether (*fl.*1828–65) specialised in moonlight scenes, including some set in Venice, in a style not at all like Turner's.

The revival of a Turnerian approach to Venice in painting was a phenomenon of the last thirty years of the nineteenth century and the first ten years of this century. At this time the artist's Venetian pictures were probably more popular than any other category of his work and they were also more frequently forged. Thanks to the display of selected items from the Turner Bequest, first at Marlborough House and then at the National Gallery, his watercolours, too, began to be known. Among those influenced by them were Albert Goodwin (1845–1932), who accompanied Ruskin to Venice in 1872, and Hercules Brabazon (1821–1906). Brabazon[54] was little more than a skilful copyist but Goodwin (fig. 14) had considerable poetic feeling though his work is slighter than Turner's and more in the manner of the Aesthetic Movement. Whistler, who claimed to despise Turner, was also probably more affected by him than he was willing to admit.

But it was in France that the most important response to Turner occurred.[55] Edmond de Goncourt was an enthusiastic admirer:

> For this Turner [a Venetian scene] is liquid gold, and within it an infusion of purple . . . Ah! this Salute, this Doge's Palace, this sea, this sky with the rose translucency of Pagodite, all as if seen in an apotheosis the colour of precious stones! And of colour in droplets, in tears, in congelations, the sort you see on the sides of vases from the Far East. For me it has the air of a painting done by a Rembrandt born in India.

By this time (1891), Félix Ziem (1812–1911) was producing Venetian views (fig. 15) in the style of Turner though with a slight Impressionist twist. Monet and Pissarro had got to know and like Turner's work in London in 1870–71 but then went off it for a while. Monet came back to it, however, when painting his views of Venice (plate 112) between 1899 and 1909. Quite how advanced his style is can be seen by comparing it with that of the American painter Thomas Moran (1837–1926),[56] who only began painting Venetian subjects (plate 110) in 1886 but did so in a manner and technique so close to Turner's that he might almost have been a younger contemporary.

The most profound impact of all, as we have already partly seen, was on the mind of Ruskin. Ruskin was attuned to responding to Venice in a way similar to Turner by two factors operating in his childhood: first, he learned to draw and to look at nature by studying books like Rogers's *Italy* and the *Landscape Annuals*, the engraved illustrations to which were after drawings by Turner himself or his early followers; second, he was steeped even more than Turner in the poetry of Byron. When he stayed in Venice for the first time in late September/early October 1835, he peppered his diary and letters with Byronic phrases – Venice is 'Like to a lovely thought in dreaming sleep', etc. – and tried his hand at Byronic verse.[57] But he had seen enough of the actual city in the course of trying to draw it to defend *Juliet and her Nurse* in his reply to *Blackwood's* the following year, with some exaggeration, as 'accurate in every particular.'

It was during his next visit, in 1841, that his point of view became most closely identified with Turner's. He had by now seen several more of the artist's Venetian paintings and had met Turner himself. 'Thank God I am here!' he wrote in his diary on arriving on 6 May. 'It is the paradise of cities and there is moon enough to make half the sanities of earth lunatic, striking its pure flashes of light against the grey water before the window.' And as he went about the city and tried once more (unsuccessfully) to draw it and (successfully) to describe it, he thought of Turner all the time.

A heavy thunder cloud came over the Doge's palace in the twilight, and rapid limitless flashes of silent lightning showed first

15. Félix Ziem, *Venice*. Oil on canvas. 97.8 × 148.6 cm. The Wallace Collection, London

behind its ridges, as the rockets rose from behind the smoke of St. Angelo [*sic*]; then retired over the Lido, lighting the whole noble group of the Salute with a bluish spectral white, as every flash touched on it with vague, mysterious gracefulness – Turner's own – the edges of the dome dark against the reflected lightning on the ground of sky.[58]

Not long after returning to London he began writing the first volume of *Modern Painters*, which was to be a hymn at once to the power and beauty of nature and the visual poetry of Turner. Into this volume, the accounts of Turner's Venetian paintings, some of which have been quoted here, fell naturally into place like the keystone of an arch.

Ruskin was never, on the other hand, to look at Venice with eyes like Turner's again. On his third visit, in 1845, he began to concern himself not with modern paintings of Venice but with Venetian paintings, and to see buildings not as features in a landscape but as artefacts. The picturesque qualities of buildings and the exhilarating Turnerian effects of sea and sky were no longer enough; and when, in 1849–50, he began researching and writing *The Stones of Venice* they were a positive distraction. *The Stones* is just that: a book which interprets the spiritual, cultural and artistic history of Venice founded on her basic constituents. Each of the separate stones of Venice – the individual pieces of carved rock, stones with a small 's' – is not only a material object, to be appreciated as such; it is also Venetian history writ small. Each stone in the façade, each bird cut into the foliated capital, each tessera in the mosaic pavement, is evidence both of the state of mind of the workman who carved it and of the spiritual temper of Venetian society.

As he wrote to his father in defence of the first volume when it was published: 'You know I promised them no Romance. I promised them stones. Not even bread. I do not *feel* any Romance in Venice. It is simply a heap of ruins . . . and *this* is the great fact which I meant to teach, – to give Turneresque descriptions of the thing would not have needed ten days study or residence'.[59]

This is not to say that Ruskin ceased to admire or to write enthusiastically about Turner's Venetian paintings and watercolours as works of art. It was just that they were no longer representative of his most urgent intellectual and moral preoccupations. Yet there was one more occasion when Turner would serve. In the passage at the beginning of volume two of *The Stones of Venice*, describing in high poetic prose the approach to the city, Ruskin simultaneously takes his leave of Turner's Venice while entering his own.

As the boat drew nearer to the city, the coast which the traveller had just left sank behind him into one long, low, sad-coloured line, tufted irregularly with brushwood and willows: . . . the chain of the Alps girded the whole horizon to the north – a wall of jagged blue, here and there showing through its clefts a wilderness of misty precipices, fading far back into the recesses of Cadore, and itself rising and breaking away eastward, where the sun struck opposite upon its snow, into mighty fragments of peaked light, standing up behind the barred clouds of evening, one after another, countless, the crown of the Adrian sea, until the eye turned back from pursuing them, to rest upon the nearer burning of the companiles of Murano, and on the great city, where it magnified itself along the waves, as the quick silent pacing of the gondola drew nearer and nearer.

NOTES

1. For an account of Venice under Austrian occupation, see the first chapter of Paul Ginsborg, *Daniele Manin and the Venetian Revolution of 1848–9*, Cambridge 1979

2. Particulars of these restorations are given in G. Gattinoni, *Il Campanile di San Marco in Venezia*, Venice 1910, pp. 112–4, cited (not quite correctly) by Hardy George, 'Turner in Venice', *Art Bulletin*, 1971, LIII, p. 85, note 6; there do not appear to have been any significant works on the Campanile between 1822 and 1839.

3. *The Letters of Percy Bysshe Shelley*, ed. F.L. Jones, Oxford 1964, vol. II, Letter no. 483 (8 October 1818, to Thomas Love Peacock).

4. There is an admirable survey of Romantic attitudes to Venice in Jeanne Clegg, *Ruskin and Venice*, London 1981, chapter 1, 'Venice the Romantic'.

5. The affinity between Turner and Byron was already noticed in Ruskin, first in his *Notes on the Turner Gallery at Marlborough House*, 1856 (*Works*, XIII, p. 143) and afterwards in *Praeterita*, 1886–89 (*ibid*, XXXV pp. 294–5). It has often been remarked on since.

6. No. 263. This is only the second quotation from Byron in the Royal Academy catalogues. In 1817, J.R. Walker had shown two paintings, probably landscapes (nos 460 and 482), illustrating scenes from *Childe Harold*, cantos II and III. The first of them was accompanied by the line, 'Monastic Zitza, from thy shady bowers'.

7. *The Letters of Edward Gibbon*, ed. J.E. Norton, London 1956, I, p. 193.

8. In these respects, if not in literary power or intensity of religious feeling, Ruskin was anticipated by the Venetian historian Count Pietro Selvatico, whose *Sulla Architettura e sulla Scultura in Venezia* appeared in 1847. The importance of this book for Ruskin's *The Stones* has not been sufficiently appreciated.

9. For Wilson, see David Solkin, *Richard Wilson*, London – Cardiff – New Haven 1982, catalogue nos 12–16. Cozens's drawing is in the first of the Beckford sketchbooks now in the Whitworth Art Gallery, Manchester; see the sale catalogue, Sotheby's, 29 November 1973, vol. I, no. 18. Mention should be made here of the obscure William James (*fl.* 1754–71) who apparently followed Canaletto back to Venice from England, settled in the city and manufactured *pastiches* of the Italian master's pictures.

10. It represents the Grand Canal seen through the arch of the Rialto Bridge looking roughly south. 177.5 × 355.5 cm. Tate Gallery, B/J 245.

11. See John Gage, 'Turner and Stourhead: the Making of a Classicist?', *Art Quarterly*, Spring 1974, pp. 77–82.

12. For a full account of this publication and Turner's involvement in it, see Cecilia Powell, 'Topography, Imagination and Travel: Turner's Relationship with James Hakewill', *Art History*, 1982, vol. V, no. 4, pp. 408–25. Both here and in her PhD thesis (Courtauld Institute of Art, University of London, 1985), Dr Powell gives further reasons for thinking that Turner had read canto IV of *Childe Harold* in 1818 and that the poem influenced his attitude to Rome as well as Venice.

13. That *The Custom House & Church of the Madonna della Salute, at the Entrance of the Grand Canal, Venice* belonged to the series was discovered by Cecilia Powell, *op.cit.*, p. 414; Hakewill's drawing is there reproduced on plate 23. *The Rialto, Venice* is W.700. Both watercolours were last recorded early this century.

14. TB CLXXI

15. TB CLXXII

16. *Ibid.*

17. See John Gage, *Collected Correspondence of J.M.W. Turner*, London 1980, p. 80, Letter 85. The date of Turner's departure can be inferred from this letter.

18. The sketchbook, TB CXCIV, recording Turner's visit to the Simplon, the dating of which puzzled A.J. Finberg (*Inventory*, p. 577), has been plausibly assigned to this moment in the artist's career by Cecilia Powell (PhD thesis, see note 12 above).

19. *In Venice with Turner*, PhD thesis (Courtauld Institute of Art, University of London, 1970), pp. 62–72. The crucial information is more clearly set out by Dr George in 'Turner in Venice', *Art Bulletin*, 1971, LIII, pp. 84–7.

20. See TB CLXXI, pp. 24f (this is the sketchbook containing Hakewill's travel notes).

21. *Modern Painters*, vol. I, 1843, from the chapter, 'General Application of the Foregoing Principles', added for the 3rd ed., 1846; *Works*, III, p. 244.

22. TB CLXXXI. As Hardy George has pointed out (PhD thesis, p. 20), a fourth sketchbook, TB CLXX, identified by A.J. Finberg as having been used by Turner in Venice in 1819, in fact has nothing to do with that city; the so-called Venetian views in this book, executed in sepia wash, all represent scenes in London, chiefly Waterloo Bridge with Somerset House in the background.

23. TB CLXXVII: from a note inside the cover.

24. Tate Gallery; B/J 228.

25. W. 725.

26. A.J. Finberg, *In Venice with Turner*, 1930, p. 73 plate XII. According to Martin Hardic, *Water-colour Painting in Britain*, vol. II, London 1967, p. 39, this watercolour then belonged to R.W. Reford, Montreal. It is not catalogued in Andrew Wilton, *The Life and Work of J.M.W. Turner*.

27. Respectively W. 718, pl. 156 (Indianapolis Museum of Art, Indiana, Kurt Pantzer Collection) and W. 721, pl. 158 (private collection).

28. Dennis Farr, *William Etty*, London 1958, pp. 38–40.

29. See note to plate 27.

30. *Works*, XII, p. 312.

31. Quoted from B/J, p. 182, under no. 349.

32. See the catalogue by Pieter van der Merwe of the exhibition, *The Spectacular Career of Clarkson Stanfield*, Sunderland (Tyne and Wear Museums) 1979, nos 127f.

33. His second Venetian exhibit of 1833, the now lost *Ducal Palace, Venice* (B/J 352), which was apparently very small, was clearly a homage to Bonington; that is, if the identification with the engraving by W. Millar of 1854 is correct, though there is some doubt about it.

34. PhD thesis, p. 84.

35. See pp. 999 and 1029.

36. For bibliographical references see note 19 above and, in addition, 'Turner in Europe in 1833', *Turner Studies*, 1984, vol. IV, no. 1, pp. 2–22.

37. See *Correspondence*, ed. cit. in note 17, Letters 193, 211, 227. All or a large part of the summers of 1831, 1832, 1834, 1836 and probably 1838 are accounted for by other trips, though an excursion to Venice in 1834 or 1836 cannot be completely ruled out.

38. *Ibid.*, Letter 236. This letter provides important confirmation of the trip.

39. Hardy George, *op. cit.* in note 19.

40. *Correspondence*, Letter 238.

41. Quoted from Hardy George, PhD thesis, p. 310, note 87.

42. See Ginsborg, *op. cit.* in note 1.

43. W. 1352–74.

44. Plates 68, 69, 73, 76, 80, 86–95.

45. This was first pointed out in the case of the three given by Ruskin to the Ashmolean Museum by Luke Herrmann, *Ruskin and Turner*, London 1968, p. 83 under no. 56.

46. Plates 58, 59, 61–7, 71, 72, 74, 75, 79, 82–4.

47. *Works*, XII. p. 151

48. See John Gage, *Colour in Turner: Poetry and Truth*, London 1969, pp. 114f.

49. Luke Herrmann, *loc. cit.* in note 45.

50. B/J 356 and 362.

51. B/J 368.

52. B/J 401, 404, 405.

53. B/J, under 412.

54. See A. Weil, *The Wide World of Hercules Brabazon Brabazon*, exhibition catalogue, Hastings Museum and Art Gallery, 1976.

55. Gage, *op. cit.* in note 48, pp. 189–95.

56. See Margaretta M. Lovell, *Venice: The American View, 1860–1920*, exhibition catalogue, San Francisco and Cleveland, 1984–5, especially pp. 66–70.

57. Clegg, *op. cit.* in note 4, pp. 36f.

58. *Ibid.*, p. 43.

59. J.L. Bradley, *Ruskin's Letters from Venice 1851–52*, New Haven 1955, Letter of 18 February 1852.

Notes on the Plates

Note

The following abbreviations are used in referring to catalogues and works of reference (full details are given in the Select Bibliography)

B/J	M. Butlin and E. Joll, *The Paintings of J.M.W. Turner*, 1977
R.	W.G. Rawlinson, *The Engraved Work of J.M.W. Turner*, 1908 and 1913
Ruskin, *Works*	E.T. Cook and Alexander Wedderburn (eds), *The Works of John Ruskin*, 39 vols, 1903–12
TB	A.J. Finberg, *A Complete Inventory of the Turner Bequest*, 1909
W.	A. Wilton, *Life and Work of J.M.W. Turner*, 1979 (catalogue of watercolours)

Titles for those paintings which were exhibited at the Royal Academy by Turner are given as they appeared in the catalogue.

Venetian place names are referred to in Italian or in English according to common usage and whichever seemed more appropriate.

I

On Lake Como   1819

Watercolour; 225 × 291 mm

TB CLXXXI-I

Turner's first visit to Italy in the summer of 1819 was the fulfilment of a long-standing interest. Since the 1790s several of his most important paintings had been inspired by the history and landscape of the country, familiar to him chiefly through the works of the great seventeenth-century landscapists, Claude, Poussin and Salvator Rosa. Sir Thomas Lawrence, writing to the diarist Joseph Farington (an early supporter of Turner) in July 1819, urged Turner to visit Italy: '. . . the subtle harmony of this atmosphere, that wraps everything in its own milky sweetness . . . can only be rendered, according to my belief, by the beauty of his tones'.

Turner was to spend four months in Italy, and the importance that he attached to this tour is shown in the quantity of studies which filled nineteen sketchbooks. There are hundreds of tiny pencil sketches recording every aspect of the landscape, architecture and appearance of the Italians, as well as details of works of art, lists of places to visit, and phrases to be learned.

While in Italy in 1819 Turner made no finished watercolours, although in both Rome and Naples he was to paint numerous coloured studies, mostly on paper prepared with a ground of grey wash. The handful of sketches he made immediately after his arrival in Italy – two views of Lake Como, four of Venice itself – are much simpler in technique, but, perhaps as a direct consequence, even more striking in effect. The delicacy and subtlety of the light palette that Turner used in this first short series of watercolours is shown in this study of Lake Como, in which the sunlight streams across the mountains and water.

2

S. Giorgio Maggiore: morning   1819

Watercolour; 224 × 287 mm

TB CLXXXI-4

Reproduced on this and the next three plates are the four views of Venice which Turner executed in watercolour in 1819. Otherwise he spent his time on this brief visit (8/9 to 12/13 September) making numerous small pencil drawings in his sketchbooks. All four compositions seem to be from viewpoints at or near the entrance to the Grand Canal and the Canale della Giudecca. With his unerring instinct for the essential visual characteristics of a place, Turner grasped at once the distinctive forms, shapes and outlines of Venice, while bringing to the task of rendering them a watercolour technique evolved in England. The outcome is a new pictorial treatment of the city, in which atmosphere and the colours of the sky and sea play a greater part than hitherto. In each of these four watercolours, the buildings are represented with the light either full on them (Pl. 5) or coming from behind. This causes the architectural details within the contour largely to disappear and the shapes to look almost flat; nevertheless the outlines of the forms are faithfully if summarily preserved, as are the spatial intervals between the different planes. In this view of S. Giorgio Maggiore, a hazy light softens the forms of the buildings and veils the sun, which adds to the magic of the effect.

To judge from the angle at which the church and monastery are seen, the view is evidently from the steps of the Palazzo Giustiniani, later to become the Hotel Europa (where Turner was to stay on subsequent visits to Venice): it is not from the Dogana as is usually said (Pl. 3 was taken from the same viewpoint). The strip of land in the distance at the left is probably the Castello district, with the campanile of S. Pietro di Castello rising from it and the Public Gardens and perhaps a part of the Lido beyond. The pale sun, more visible from its reflection in the water than from its image in the sky, has risen about two hours above the horizon.

3

The Punta della Salute, with the Zitelle in the distance: morning   1819

Watercolour; 224 × 287 mm

TB CLXXXI-6

The view shown in this watercolour is taken from the same point as plate 2, that is the steps of, or close beside, the Palazzo Giustiniani (later the Hotel Europa) on the S. Marco side of the entrance to the Grand Canal. In fact, when the two compositions are placed side by side, with plate 3 on the right, they would almost join up. They are identical in style and must have been executed one immediately after the other, about two hours after sunrise.

The building in the centre is the Dogana and the one beyond it on the Giudecca the church of the Zitelle (properly, S. Maria della Presentazione; *zitelle* means 'unmarried women'), and not, as has been supposed, the Redentore.

4

Looking east from the Giudecca: early morning (?)   1819

Watercolour; 224 × 286 mm

TB CLXXXI-5

Of the four watercolours made by Turner during his first visit to Venice in 1819 this is the simplest and most understated, yet is perhaps the one which most perfectly captures the evanescent beauty of the city seen from a distance, recalling Shelley's lines:

> Underneath Day's azure eyes
> Ocean's nursling, Venice lies . . .
> Lo! The sun upsprings behind
> Broad, red, radiant, half-reclined
> On the level quivering line
> of the Waters crystalline
>
> (*Lines written among the Euganean Hills*, 1818)

For all its poetic truth, however, this watercolour is topographically the most puzzling of the four. There is no point either within the area of Venice itself (such as the entrance to the Canale della Giudecca) or out on the Lagoon from which such a view can be seen. The tall tower is suggestive of the Campanile of St Mark's and the line of buildings on the horizon recalls the long curved waterfront which stretches from the Piazzetta along the Riva degli Schiavoni and past the Public Gardens to S. Elena. However, if this is what is represented, many architectural details are wrong or omitted, and any view taken from far enough away to correspond with the scale of the buildings, particularly those on the left, would in reality be blocked by the Giudecca and S. Giorgio Maggiore. Perhaps Turner was recalling a sunrise – or, for that matter, sunset – which he had seen across the Lagoon, and combined this with an 'ideal' view of the famous waterfront reconstructed from memory. Assuming that this is correct and that the watercolour was not executed from nature, it is striking how close it is in style to plates 2 and 3, which there is every reason to believe were done directly from the motif.

5

The Campanile of St Mark's and the Ducal Palace 1819

Watercolour over pencil; 224 × 289 mm

TB CLXXXI-7

In its bold, almost block-like treatment of architectural forms, this sheet contrasts with the refined delicacy of the other watercolours made by Turner on his first visit to the city (Pls 2–4). The fact that the details were first drawn accurately, if summarily, in pencil makes it possible, though by no means certain, that the colour was added afterwards, away from the motif. The simplified palette, confined to blues and yellows, is consistent with this. By ignoring the brick red of the Campanile and the subtle rose tint of the upper part of the Ducal Palace, Turner allowed himself to create a design that is as much expressive as descriptive: expressive, that is, of the blaze of sunlight falling on the buildings shortly before noon. The intense blue sky, too, is filled with late morning heat. Like Monet, who was in Venice ninety years later, Turner here paints the dazzling light reflected from objects rather than the objects themselves – though one is equally reminded in this instance of an often-quoted remark made by Hazlitt a few years

earlier about Turner himself: that his pictures were 'representations not properly of the objects of nature as of the medium through which they are seen'.

It is tempting to think that plates 2, 3 and 5 represent, in that order, some two hours work between 9 and 11 during a single morning, whether or not plate 5 was actually coloured from nature. The viewpoint is from the steps of S. Giorgio Maggiore or a boat resting between S. Giorgio and the Molo.

6

The Ducal Palace *c*.1827

Watercolour vignette with scratching-out over touches of pencil; 123 × 183 mm on a sheet of paper 240 × 306 mm

Engraved by Edward Goodall 1830

TB CCLXXX-193 (W.1162)

Samuel Rogers (1763–1855), banker, collector and amateur poet, had originally published his long poem *Italy* in two parts, the first in 1822, the second in 1828, but neither met with much success, and before the second part was issued Rogers had already decided to bring out a new edition with illustrations. His desire to secure Turner's services made him ready to offer a considerable sum for each drawing, but in the event Turner hired them out for a fee on the understanding that they were later to be returned to him. Work on the illustrations was in progress by 1827, and the series was largely completed by the late summer of 1828. The book was published in 1830 and was immediately successful. Among its many readers was the enchanted thirteen year old Ruskin, who recalled years later in his autobiography that 'this was the first means I had of looking carefully at Turner's work, and I might not without some appearance of reason attribute to this gift the entire direction of my life's energies'. In 1852 he wrote to Rogers that whenever his feelings for Venice became hostile 'I used to read over a little bit of the "Venice" in the *Italy*, and it put me always into the right tone of thought again'.

Turner's designs for the Italian subjects were worked up from drawings made during his first visit to Italy in 1819; both the *Milan to Venice* and *Venice to Ancona* sketchbooks (TB CLXXV and TB CLXXVI) include similar views of the Ducal Palace as does one of the 1819 watercolours (Pl. 5).

95

Now the scene shifts to Venice—to a square
Glittering with light, all nations masking there,
With light reflected on the tremulous tide,
Where gondolas in gay confusion glide,
Answering the jest, the song on every side;

16. Edward Goodall after J.M.W. Turner, *The Rialto – Moonlight*. 1833.
Engraving (R.386). 92 × 83 mm

7
The Rialto: moonlight   *c.*1832

Watercolour vignette; 118 × 135 mm on a sheet of paper
241 × 305 mm

Engraved by William Miller 1833 (fig. 16)

TB CCLXXX-196 (W.1190)

Following the success of Turner's illustrated edition of Rogers's *Italy* and as the result of the friendship that had developed between artist and poet during their first collaboration, Turner undertook a second commission to illustrate a series of poems by Rogers. Thirty-three designs were engraved after watercolours by Turner in 1833 and the volume was published in 1834. As with *Italy*, Turner agreed to lend the drawings to the engravers for a fee from Rogers, and they were later returned to him, subsequently forming part of the Bequest.

The source for this watercolour vignette, an illustration to Rogers's poem *Human Life*, is to be found in Turner's pencil sketches of Venice made in 1819. The *Milan to Venice* sketchbook (TB CLXXV) includes a sequence of drawings made along the Grand Canal, approaching and then looking back at the Rialto (pp. 73 to 84); a preparatory drawing specifically for this watercolour is TB CCLXXX-108. Turner's illustration is a haunting moonlit view:

> Now the scene shifts to Venice – to a square
> Glittering with light, all nations masking there,
> With light reflected on the tremulous tide,
> Where gondolas in gay confusion glide . . .

8

St Mark's from the Piazzetta   1833?

Watercolour and bodycolour on brown paper; 150 × 226 mm

TB CCCXVIII-1

9

The Piazzetta: night   1833?

Watercolour and bodycolour on brown paper; 149 × 227 mm

TB CCCXIX-2

Among the most distinctive of Turner's Venetian studies is a sequence on brown paper. They have in the past been associated with Turner's second visit to Venice, but more recently it has been suggested that all the Venetian watercolours (with the exception of those which undoubtedly date from 1819, plates 2–5) should be assigned to his third and last visit of 1840, or shortly afterwards. However, given the very marked differences between the various groups, both in mood and style, it seems improbable that they were all executed at the same time. The series on brown paper seems to relate fairly convincingly to the themes which interested Turner in the 1830s – the dramatic contrasts of light and dark, for example – and are here tentatively reassigned to the period of Turner's second visit to Venice in 1833. Although a direct connection has been denied by various scholars, several of the sheets in this sequence appear to be related to the genesis of the painting *Juliet and her Nurse* (Pl. 97), exhibited in 1836, again suggesting that they date from 1833 rather than 1840.

These studies, both in the treatment of the architecture and in the procession of figures apparently dressed in the red Senatorial robes of pre-Revolutionary Venice, are reminiscent of the compositions of the famous Venetian view painters, notably Canaletto and Guardi. However, the presence of a soldier standing beside a cannon and a sentry-box (Pl. 8) is a reminder of the Austrian occupation of Venice: Ruskin was to complain in 1845 of the jarring effect of their silhouettes against the arcade of the Ducal Palace. In plate 9, a crowd seems to be gathered around a puppet or Punch and Judy show: a similar motif occurs on the left-hand side of *Juliet and her Nurse*.

10

Moonlight   1833?

Watercolour and bodycolour on greyish-brown paper; 215 × 287 mm

TB CCCXVIII-3

With a few summary touches of colour Turner conjures up a moonlit night on the Lagoon.

> . . . the dash
> Phosphoric of the oar, or rapid twinkle
> Of the far lights of skimming gondolas
>
> (Byron, *Marino Faliero*, 1820)

11

An open-air theatre (?)   1833?

Watercolour and bodycolour on brown paper; 225 × 292 mm

Inscribed *verso*: 1

TB CCCXVIII-4

Among the group of studies on brown paper are a number that seem to show a play in progress; whether these were made on the spot or from memory soon afterwards is uncertain, but the generalisation of forms, combined with their boldness of treatment, suggests that they were drawn in sequence. This is one of the more mysterious in the series; the blaze of vermilion on the left suggests a fire.

12

The Campanile of St Mark's from the roof of the Hotel Europa: lightning   1833?

Watercolour and bodycolour on brown paper; 159 × 231 mm

Inscribed *verso*: *5*

TB CCCXIX-6

13

The Campanile of St Mark's from the roof of the Hotel Europa: moonlight   1833?

Watercolour and bodycolour on brown paper; 241 × 308 mm

Inscribed *verso*: *2*

TB CCCXVIII-5

Turner made a number of studies of the view from the roof-top or from the window of an upper room of the Hotel Europa where he certainly stayed in 1840 and possibly also during his previous visit in 1833. In the past, these studies have been associated with the composition of Turner's painting *Juliet and her Nurse*, exhibited at the Royal Academy in 1836 (Pl. 97), but more recently any specific connection has been discounted. However, the fact that elements in both of these sheets and those illustrated on plates 28 and 29 (as well perhaps as Pls 9 and 74) are echoed in the design of *Juliet and her Nurse* suggests that they pre-date 1836. The view over the roofs of the Procuratie Nuove looking towards the Campanile in the painting is so distinctive that it is difficult to ignore such connections. It is certainly true that Turner was in the habit of going back to subjects that had interested him in earlier years, and re-drawing them. To have returned to any one element in *Juliet and her Nurse* in 1840 would be in character, but it is surely unlikely that he would have repeated three such elements – namely, the firework displays (Pls 28, 29), the puppet show (Pl. 9) and these roof-top views.

14

The interior of St Mark's   1833?

Watercolour and bodycolour on brown paper; 295 × 223 mm

Inscribed *verso*: *8*

TB CCCXVIII-7

15

The interior of St Mark's   1833?

Watercolour and bodycolour on brown paper; 314 × 243 mm

Inscribed *verso*: *10*

TB CCCXVIII-8

These two studies are unusual among Turner's Venetian watercolours in showing the interior of St Mark's. Canaletto had also represented the interior of the cathedral and for him, too, it was an unusual subject. Whether Turner knew of Canaletto's paintings – one of which (Royal Collection) is of the same view as plate 14 looking towards the north transept, with the rood-screen on the right – is, however, uncertain. The interior of St Mark's was becoming of increasing interest in the 1830s to artists of a more Gothic persuasion, such as Samuel Prout, as it became later – and supremely – for Ruskin. Turner's two watercolours may very faintly reflect this interest but it is characteristic of him to ignore, unlike Prout, the architectural detail and to concentrate on the shafts of light penetrating the mysterious darkness of the church.

16

The Dogana from the steps of the Hotel Europa
1833?

Watercolour and bodycolour on brown paper; 232 × 312 mm

Inscribed *verso*: *25*

TB CCXVIII-19

17

The Dogana and S. Maria della Salute from the Molo   1833?

Watercolour and bodycolour on buff paper; 222 × 304 mm

Inscribed *verso*: *17*

TB CCCXVIII-13

Two views taken from closely adjacent points: plate 16 shows the Dogana silhouetted against a delicate blue and pink sky, probably from the steps of the Hotel Europa, or from the nearby Calle del Ridotto. Plate 17, a moonlit scene, is from a viewpoint nearer the entrance of the Grand Canal – perhaps on the quay in front of the Giardino Reale. Plate 29, a firework display in which rockets shoot up into the sky above the Dogana, must have been taken from the same position.

18

A procession, perhaps in the Piazza (?)   1833?

Watercolour and bodycolour on brown paper; 225 × 292 mm

Inscribed *verso*: *18*

TB CCCXVIII-14

This sheet, like plates 8 and 9, seems to be a reminiscence of paintings of the Piazza by Canaletto and Guardi. There may also be echoes of Bonington's late Venetian pictures: his *Ducal Palace with a religious procession* had been exhibited in London in 1828 to considerable acclaim. However, Turner's treatment of a similar subject is quite different in mood and style, consisting as it does of the most summary indications of form, and is a study made solely for his own reference.

19

An interior   1833?

Watercolour and bodycolour on buff paper; 226 × 294 mm

Inscribed *verso*: *11*

TB CCCXVIII-9

20

The interior of a theatre (?)   1833?

Watercolour and bodycolour on buff paper; 224 × 293 mm

Inscribed *verso*: *24*

TB CCCXVIII-18

Both these sheets are from a small group of drawings which seem to show the interior of a theatre or to be recollections of a play in progress (see Pls 11 and 21). The dark-toned paper and sweeping highlights of opaque bodycolour are perfectly suited to such subjects, which Turner clearly found exciting.

21

The lovers: a scene from 'The Merchant of Venice' (?)   1833?

Watercolour and bodycolour on brown paper; 239 × 314 mm

TB CCCXVIII-20

The identification of this subject as a scene from *The Merchant of Venice* or another play was made by A.J. Finberg, perhaps because two other studies on brown paper, plates 11 and 20, seem to show theatres, thus suggesting that Turner was noting his recollections of a visit to a play. Although it is unlikely that Shakespeare's *The Merchant of Venice* was being performed in Venice at this date, it is not necessary to suppose that it was in order for Turner to have depicted a scene from it here. This play seems to have been so closely associated with Venice in his mind that he was quite capable of imagining it being staged in the streets of Venice. The resulting element of fantasy gives a particular character to the present sheet and to one or two other figure compositions in the same series.

22

A bridge   1833?

Watercolour and bodycolour on brown paper; 226 × 292 mm

Inscribed *verso*: 29

TB CCCXVIII-23

23

A wineshop   1833?

Watercolour and bodycolour on brown paper; 234 × 308 mm

Inscribed *verso*: 27

TB CCCXVIII-21

Many of the drawings in this series are glimpses along mysterious *calli* and narrow canals or into dark interiors, rapid sketches dashed on to the paper with extraordinary freedom of handling and economy of means. In plate 22, for instance, the steps of the bridge are convincingly suggested with just a calligraphic trail of white bodycolour and a few touches of black wash.

24

The Campanile, from the Atrio of the Palazzo Reale   1833?

Watercolour and bodycolour on brown paper; 308 × 237 mm

TB CCCXVIII-26

The Campanile of St Mark's is seen here from the arcade of the Palazzo Reale (now the Ala Napoleonica), framed by one of the arches: such dramatic designs are characteristic of the series. The upper part of the Campanile is not visible, so it is impossible to tell whether there was scaffolding in place when Turner made this drawing: the dating of these brown paper sketches is to some extent affected by the fact that repairs took place in 1840, but apparently not in 1833 (see Pl. 30). One would therefore not expect to see signs of scaffolding if these were drawn in 1833 or shortly afterwards as reminiscences of the artist's visit to Venice.

25

The Ducal Palace: the Porta della Carta   1833?

Watercolour and bodycolour on buff paper; 297 × 234 mm

TB CCCXVIII-28

In contrast to the studies of the famous vistas of Venice painted on white paper – the Lagoon, the Grand Canal and the Bacino – many of those on brown paper are of a single architectural feature. This is one such drawing, notable also for its rich and decorative colour – an effect enhanced by the tone of the paper. This view is taken from the same spot as plate 30, but with the artist facing in the opposite direction. The Porta della Carta, designed by Bartolomeo and Giovanni Bon and built between 1438 and 1442, was so named because it was there that the 'carte' (papers) announcing new laws were posted. The rather vignette-like treatment of the subject with the emphasis on a darker central feature looks forward to some of the etchings of Venice made by Whistler (fig. 17).

26

View through medieval arches on to a moonlit canal   1833?

Watercolour and bodycolour on brown paper; 306 × 237 mm

TB CCCXVIII-27

Several drawings in this series make dramatic use of arches to frame buildings, or as here, to create a particularly effective silhouette against the moonlit sky. With only the most rapid touches of bodycolour Turner conjures up reflections in the dark waters of a canal.

Prolonged periods of exhibition in the past have resulted in damage from light, causing the paper to change colour (and hence the tonal balance has also altered): the original colour can be seen at the edges of the sheet.

27

The Bridge of Sighs: night   1833?

Watercolour and bodycolour on brown paper; 227 × 153 mm

TB CCCXIX-5

Together with the other studies on brown paper, this is here tentatively dated c.1833; however, there seems to be a more than coincidental relationship between this sheet and a painting by William Etty (1787–1849), *The Bridge of Sighs* (fig. 5), exhibited at the Royal Academy in 1835. Etty had visited Venice in 1823, and an extract from his description of former practices in the State Prisons was printed in the Academy's exhibition catalogue; the painting showed the moment after the execution of a criminal had occurred, when the body was removed in order to be disposed of in the Lagoon. The same incident can just be made out in Turner's watercolour. W.C. Macready, the celebrated actor who bought Etty's painting in 1840, wrote: 'It is to me poetry on canvas. The story of that gloomy canal and its fatal bridge is told at once; there is a history before you, and a commentary upon it in the single star that is looking down upon the dark deeds below', a symbolism which Turner's watercolour seems to share.

28

Fireworks on the Molo   1833?

Watercolour and bodycolour with touches of white chalk on brown paper; 226 × 299 mm

Inscribed *verso*: 12

TB CCCXVIII-10

29

S. Maria della Salute: night scene with rockets
1833?

Watercolour and bodycolour on brown paper; 239 × 315 mm

TB CCCXVIII-29

During the mid-1830s and early 1840s Turner became increasingly interested in exploring the most dramatic pictorial effects of light and

17. James Abbott McNeill Whistler, *Two Doorways, Venice*. 1880. Etching. 203 × 292 mm. Kennedy 193

shade, and produced a number of paintings and watercolours on this theme. Among the most spectacular of these are the two paintings of the fire that, in 1834, destroyed the old Houses of Parliament (an event witnessed by Turner) and *Keelmen heaving in Coals by Night*, a moonlit industrial scene on the River Tyne, all exhibited in 1835. In the following year he exhibited *Juliet and her Nurse* (Pl. 97), another moonlit setting, in which the sky is irradiated by flashes of phosphorescent light from a display of fireworks. Like the rest of the Venetian studies made on brown paper, plates 28 and 29 were formerly assigned to Turner's second visit to the city (then assumed to have taken place in 1835) and were thought to be related to *Juliet and her Nurse*. More recently, they have been connected with his visit of 1840. It is here tentatively suggested that they should be reassigned to his second visit in 1833, for it seems hardly coincidental that almost exactly the same scene as plate 28 should occur in the background of *Juliet and her Nurse*.

Turner's combination of a dark-toned ground and bodycolour is perfectly suited to the subject: the paper is left bare in places – on the façade of the Salute for example – and he uses only a few colours: blue, touches of red and black, and, most dramatically, white for the cupola of the Salute, gleaming in the reflected light, and for the plumes of sparks from the fireworks, which shoot up into the inky darkness of the night.

30

The Campanile of St Mark's with the Pilastri Acritani, from the Porta della Carta 1840?

Watercolour with bodycolour over pencil on grey paper; 282 × 192 mm

TB CCCXVII-19

This drawing shows the Campanile of St Mark's with the Pilastri Acritani (two pillars brought to Venice as trophies from Acre in the thirteenth century) viewed from the Porta della Carta (see Pl. 25); to the left of the Campanile is the Libreria Sansoviniana, and in the left foreground a corner of the Ducal Palace.

The upper part of the Campanile is shown covered with scaffolding, a fact which suggests that this drawing can be dated 1840 rather than

1833; extensive repairs were carried out in 1840. From the fifteenth century onwards the Campanile has undergone structural problems, having been struck by lightning and earthquakes on several occasions. In 1902 it collapsed completely and spectacularly, but was rebuilt according to its original appearance between 1903 and 1912. According to Gregorio Gattinoni, *Il Campanile di S. Marco*, 1910, scaffolding was in place during the following years which are relevant to the dating of Turner's Venetian drawings: 1819–20 (a small platform around the spire), and from November 1838 to 22 December 1840. While Turner might have shown the Campanile without scaffolding, for aesthetic reasons, particularly in more finished works, it would be uncharacteristic of him to show scaffolding if it was not in place. Several pencil studies in the *Rotterdam and Venice* sketchbook (TB CCCXX-88 and *ante*), which has been dated 1840 on external evidence, show the Campanile with scaffolding around it.

31

The entrance to the Grand Canal with the Campanile and the Ducal Palace 1840?

Pencil, watercolour and red chalk on grey paper; 189 × 280 mm

TB CCCXVII-5

The series of Venetian studies on grey paper (see Pls 30–42) were related by A.J. Finberg to Turner's second visit to the city, chiefly on the ground that he was using bodycolour extensively at that period (in his drawings for the *Rivers of France* and in the *Petworth* series, for example). However, they are very different in character from the other group of Venetian studies in bodycolour on brown paper (see Pls 8–29). There are topographical indications to suggest that the grey paper series should be dated to 1840 (see Pl. 30), as well as a connection between some of the drawings and the *Rotterdam and Venice* sketchbook (TB CCCXX), which can certainly be dated 1840.

The rapid, almost shorthand, character of the drawing in many of these studies seems to suggest that at least some of them were sketched on the spot.

32

The Dogana, Campanile of St Mark's and the Ducal Palace   1840?

Watercolour and bodycolour over pencil on grey paper;
193 × 281 mm

Inscribed bottom left: *8 V*

TB CCCXVII-20

One of Turner's favourite views, this is taken from the Giudecca, with the Dogana on the left, and the Riva degli Schiavoni as far as the Pietà to the right. The Campanile is shown without scaffolding (which was in place in 1840), but Turner probably just decided to omit it and to draw what he knew to be the architecture beneath.

The inscription suggests that Turner may have been contemplating a series of finished watercolours of Venetian subjects: there are similar inscriptions on Swiss studies of the early 1840s – on many of the Lucerne series for example (TB CCCLXIV-182-3, 192, 196 etc.), which are annotated with an *L* and a serial number, several of which Turner then developed into finished watercolours for particular patrons.

33

S. Maria della Salute and the Dogana from the Zitelle, with the Campanile of S. Stefano beyond   1840?

Watercolour and bodycolour with pen over pencil on grey paper;
191 × 281 mm

TB CCCXVII-21

This drawing is similar in style and technique to one in the Fitzwilliam Museum, *Venice from the Lagoon* (W. 1362); both may have been taken from much the same viewpoint, although looking in different directions, and both concentrate in particular on the boats and fishermen in the foreground.

34

The steps of S. Maria della Salute, the Campanile of St Mark's on the left   1840?

Watercolour over pencil, with blue and black chalks, on grey paper;
184 × 278 mm

TB CCCXVII-23

In composition, this watercolour closely resembles the painting exhibited by Turner at the Royal Academy in 1835, *Venice, from the Porch of Madonna della Salute* (Metropolitan Museum, New York; B/J 362; see fig. 11). However, if these studies on grey paper do date from 1840 then clearly the relationship between this sheet and the painting is coincidental. The Campanile is shown without the scaffolding which was in place in 1840, but Turner could simply have omitted it for aesthetic reasons.

35

S. Giorgio Maggiore with the Dogana   1840?

Watercolour and bodycolour over pencil, with touches of red and black chalk on grey paper; 194 × 281 mm

TB CCCXVII-22

A view probably taken from the quay in front of the Dogana, looking across to the façade of S. Giorgio Maggiore. As in many of the sheets in this particular series, Turner makes effective use of the grey paper to suggest both sky and water.

36

The Grand Canal looking towards the Rialto   1840?

Pencil, watercolour and bodycolour with pen and ink on grey paper;
196 × 281 mm

TB CCCXVII-27

Turner drew and painted this famous view several times, and his various renditions make instructive comparisons. The *Milan to Venice* sketchbook used by Turner in 1819 includes a drawing (TB CLXXV-72 *verso* and 73) which later provided the basis for a watercolour painted after his return to London (Pantzer Collection, Indianapolis, W. 718). In the watercolour, Turner altered the proportions of the buildings, making them look rather higher, reduced the width of the Grand Canal and brought the Rialto nearer to the spectator. In 1837 he exhibited an oil painting, *The Grand Canal, Venice* (Huntington Library and Art Gallery; fig. 12), also based on the 1819 drawing, but again with considerable liberties in the treatment of the architecture, making the Palazzo Grimani (the large building on the right) even more massive, and exaggerating the sense of distance by pushing the Rialto further away.

The present drawing is from the series on grey paper probably datable *c.*1840 and thus not a study for the painting exhibited in 1837. Precise topographical accuracy is not Turner's aim here, and his treatment of architectural detail is summary. The Palazzo Grimani again dominates the foreground, but the general relationship of the buildings one to another, and the scale of the composition, are nearer to the drawing he made in 1819.

37

View on a cross-canal near the Arsenal (?) 1840?
Watercolour and bodycolour over pencil with touches of pen and ink on grey paper; 191 × 280 mm

TB CCCXVII-29

A pencil study of the same view is in the *Venice and Botzen* sketchbook of 1840, TB CCCXIII-57 *verso*, and is further confirmation that the series of studies on grey paper should be related to Turner's 1840 visit to Venice. Like several other watercolours from TB CCCXVII (see Pls 39 and 40), this is comparatively highly finished, suggesting that Turner did not paint it on the spot, but developed it from the pencil sketch either in the evening at his hotel or shortly after his return to England.

38

The Grand Canal above the Rialto, with the Ca'd'Oro (?) 1840?
Watercolour and bodycolour over pencil on grey paper; 191 × 280 mm

TB CCCXVII-28

Although the buildings are indicated only summarily, Turner seems to be looking across the Grand Canal from the corner of the quay between the Pescheria and the Palazzo Brandolin towards the Ca'd'Oro (on the extreme right) – the most important secular Gothic building in the city after the Ducal Palace, the clumsy 'restoration' of which in the mid-1840s was to cause Ruskin such distress. To the left of the Ca'd'Oro is the Palazzo Giusti and the Palazzo Fontana. This sheet is unusual among Turner's Venetian watercolours in the inclusion of a prominent figure in the foreground.

39

The Palazzo Tasca-Papafava 1840?
Watercolour and bodycolour on grey paper; 194 × 281 mm

TB CCCXVII-31

40

The Ponte della Guerra with the Palazzo Tasca-Papafava beyond 1840?
Watercolour and bodycolour on grey paper; 192 × 275 mm

Verso: a sketch in pencil and white bodycolour of the view as seen in TB CCCXVII-31

TB CCCXVII-30

A number of the watercolours on grey paper have a more deliberately topographical character and are more elaborately coloured than others in the series. This may suggest that they were worked up at a later stage from slighter sketches, such as the pencil study on the *verso* of TB CCCXVII-30. In these watercolours Turner has moved away from the open vistas of the Grand Canal and the Bacino to the mysterious and maze-like area between the Piazza San Marco and the Rialto. Plates 39 and 40 both show the Palazzo Tasca-Papafava, with its handsome early sixteenth-century doorway; plate 40 also includes the Ponte della Guerra, so called because it was one of several bridges on which two rival factions of the populace, the Castellani and the Nicolotti, used to indulge in street brawls during the Middle Ages – a rivalry expressed in the nineteenth century in competition for prizes in the regatta.

41

S. Stefano   1840?

Watercolour and bodycolour on grey paper; 279 × 191 mm

TB CCCXVII-32

A rapid pencil drawing in the *Rotterdam and Venice* sketchbook (TB CCCXX-91 *verso*), inscribed *Ponte Maurizio*, shows the nearer of the two bridges to be seen in this watercolour; since Andrew Wilton has established that TB CCCXX belongs to Turner's continental tour of 1840, this sheet and other comparable studies must therefore – if he used the sketchbook for reference when making the watercolour – be dated 1840 or later. The degree of elaboration tends to suggest that this sheet was not drawn on the spot, but executed from memory.

42

A bedroom in Venice   1840?

Watercolour and bodycolour on grey paper; 230 × 301 mm

Inscribed *verso*: *JMWT Bedroom at Venice* and *F*(?)

TB CCCXVII-34

As Turner's inscription tells us, this is a sketch of his bedroom, presumably at the Hotel Europa where he is known to have stayed during his visit to Venice in 1840 between 20 August and 3 September. The Europa was situated near the entrance to the Grand Canal, and many of Turner's favourite viewpoints were thus nearby. He made several studies of the roofscape of the city from the Europa (see Pl. 56), and in this sketch the Campanile of St Mark's (apparently, however, without the scaffolding that was in place in 1840) can be seen through the window. The immediacy of this study suggests that it must have been sketched on the spot: it recalls some of the studies of bedrooms at Petworth drawn by Turner in the late 1820s.

43

A campanile and other buildings, with a fishing boat   1840?

Watercolour; 222 × 320 mm

TB CCCXV-9

The problem of dating Turner's later Venetian drawings and watercolours is far from resolved, not least because of the uncertainty concerning the years in which he visited the city (see the Introduction). Among the Venetian studies in the Bequest is a group of twenty-one watercolours originally bound in a soft-backed sketchbook (thus known as a 'roll sketchbook'), TB CCCXV, watermarked 1834. Since it is now generally accepted that Turner's second visit to Venice took place in 1833 (it was formerly thought to have been in 1835), TB CCCXV is presumably therefore connected with his last documented visit in 1840. Stylistically, the sheets from the roll sketchbook accord with other watercolours of the early 1840s, and provide a basis on which to date other Venetian watercolours; many of the loose sheets grouped under

TB CCCXVI and others outside the Bequest share similarities of technique and colouring with those from TB CCCXV. Within the group of watercolours from the roll sketchbook there are wide variations of style and mood, suggesting that Turner was deliberately exploring a range of responses to the city and its setting. He probably used several sketchbooks simultaneously, to judge from the fact that studies sharing similar colour combinations and techniques occur both in TB CCCXV and among the loose sheets: the aquamarine, clear blue and orange-pink colours of this study, for instance, occur in various watercolours from TB CCCXVI.

It is extremely difficult to identify the topography of such generalised studies as this, in which Turner's concern is above all in capturing transient effects of light and colour. It has been suggested that it shows the Riva degli Schiavoni, perhaps with the Campanile of S. Giuseppe di Castello (presumably in the distance on the far right); the central campanile could thus, perhaps, be that of S. Giorgio dei Greci, and the dome and campanile slightly to the right could represent S. Pietro.

44

On the Grand Canal looking towards the Rialto
1840?

Watercolour over touches of pencil; 221 × 321 mm

TB CCCXV-2

Although described by C.F. Bell in his annotations to A.J. Finberg's *In Venice with Turner*, 1930, as a view of the Rialto bridge from the north, the topographical evidence suggests that it is taken from the south; a comparison with plate 60, for example, shows the same relationship of architectural elements. The campanile seems to be that of S. Bartolomeo which would have to be on the left if seen from the north. As so often in his Venetian watercolours, Turner indicates forms in a very summary but expressive fashion: here, the almost calligraphic treatment of the boats in the foreground is one of the most striking characteristics of the sheet.

45

The Grand Canal, with S. Maria della Salute on the left 1840?

Watercolour over touches of pencil; 222 × 323 mm

TB CCCXV-5

This watercolour was at one time mistakenly identified by A.J. Finberg as a preliminary study made in connection with the painting exhibited by Turner at the Royal Academy in 1835, *Venice from the Porch of Madonna della Salute* (Metropolitan Museum, New York; see fig. 11). However, since Turner's second visit to Venice has now been re-dated to 1833 and since this sketchbook is watermarked 1834, it is more likely that the present watercolour is related to his third and last visit, made in 1840. Additionally, this view is taken looking towards the Rialto rather than, as in the painting, towards the Dogana. Turner has considerably narrowed the width of the Grand Canal and overemphasised the scale of the gondolas in relation to the buildings.

46

The Grand Canal, with S. Simeone Piccolo: dusk
1840?

Watercolour; 222 × 320 mm

TB CCCXV-8

A comparatively highly finished sheet from the roll sketchbook, of the type that Turner might later have considered developing into a finished watercolour.

Turner's viewpoint appears to be midstream in the Grand Canal, not far from the entrance to Cannaregio, looking towards Santa Chiara. On the left is S. Simeone Piccolo, described somewhat unfairly by Ruskin as, 'One of the ugliest churches in Venice or elsewhere. Its black dome, like an unusual species of gasometer, is the admiration of modern Italian architects.'

47

Looking down the Grand Canal towards the Casa Corner and S. Maria della Salute   1840?

Watercolour over indications in pencil; 221 × 325 mm

Inscribed lower left: *BAIDI* (?)

TB CCCXV-6

With only the lightest of brush strokes, Turner conjures up the palazzi lining the Grand Canal, drawn with a confidence that reminds us of his earliest training as an architectural topographer. This very view had been painted by Canaletto, and Turner would have been familiar with the engravings made by Antonio Visentini after Canaletto's views of the Grand Canal, if not with a painted version of this composition (several were in British collections). In the middle distance, the cupolas and campanile of S. Maria della Salute are silhouetted against the sky, and the masts of ships can be seen in the Bacino. At the left is the Palazzo Corner della Ca'Grande ('One of the worst and coldest buildings of the central Renaissance', according to Ruskin), designed by Jacopo Sansovino in 1532, now the Prefecture, and on the extreme right, the corner of the Palazzo Barbarigo. Ruskin noted Turner's emphasis in this watercolour on the contrasting materials, the tawny brick and tiles compared with the white marble, which he thought so characteristic of Venice.

48

Moonrise, the Giudecca and the Zitelle in the distance   1840?

Watercolour; 221 × 319 mm

TB CCCXV-10

One of the most exquisite of the Venetian watercolours, particularly in its colouring and numinous atmosphere. The topographical identification is uncertain: the campanile in the foreground may be that of S. Zaccaria, rising above the cloister of the church (although Turner has placed this group of buildings nearer the Riva than in reality); the view would thus be to the west, with the Giudecca in the distance. If this is so, Turner must surely be showing the moon setting in the early morning, rather than moonrise.

49

The Giudecca   1840?

Watercolour; 221 × 321 mm

TB CCCXV-11

50

The Giudecca from the Lagoon   1840?

Watercolour; 221 × 321 mm

TB CCCXV-12

These two sheets are among the most beautiful of Turner's Venetian watercolours, irradiated with colour and reflected light, so that the distant buildings, the water and the boats seem to dissolve into a shimmering, opalescent mist (see also Pl. 62, a comparable sheet). Ruskin's description of a Venetian oil painting by Turner (probably the *Campo Santo*, Pl. 102) applies equally to watercolours such as these: 'Detail after detail, thought beyond thought, you find and feel ... the radiant mystery, inexhaustible as indistinct, beautiful, but never all revealed; secret in fulness, confused in symmetry, as nature herself is to the bewildered and foiled glance, giving out of that indistinctness, and through that confusion, the perpetual newness of the infinite, and the beautiful' (*Works*, III, p. 257).

51

The Giudecca, looking towards Fusina   1840?

Watercolour over pencil with touches of red and black chalk; 221 × 323 mm

TB CCCXV-13

Described by Ruskin as the original sketch for Turner's oil painting, *St Benedetto looking towards Fusina* (fig. 10), exhibited at the Royal Academy in 1843, this is an unusual case of a watercolour study being used as the immediate model for a painting. A less direct correspondence can be seen between plate 95 and the painting *The Sun of Venice going to sea*, plate 103, but Turner's working method at this stage of his life was never dependent on sequences of preparatory studies.

Whether this watercolour was painted during the 1840 visit to Venice or whether it should be dated rather later, when Turner was working on the composition of *St Benedetto*, is uncertain. As Andrew Wilton has pointed out, the technique of this drawing, with its mixture of watercolour and chalk, shares similarities with several of the Swiss drawings of around 1841.

52

S. Maria della Salute and the Dogana   1840?
Watercolour with touches of black chalk; 221 × 320 mm

TB CCCXV-14

53

S. Maria della Salute and the Dogana : sunset
1840?
Watercolour; 221 × 322 mm

TB CCCXV-17

54

On the Grand Canal   1840?
Watercolour over touches of pencil; 221 × 320 mm

TB CCCXV-21

A number of watercolours from the roll sketchbook share similarities of mood and treatment with these three sheets, which are essentially studies of light effects. Plate 53, a lemon yellow sunset, shows the Dogana and Salute from a similar, though closer viewpoint, than plate 52 – perhaps an early morning study.

55

The Rialto, the Palazzo Balbi on the left   1840?
Watercolour over pencil; 223 × 327 mm

TB CCCXV-20

This sheet shares similarities of colour and handling with the view of the Grand Canal illustrated on plate 54. Although Turner's treatment of architecture is here very summary, he seems to be looking towards the Rialto with the Palazzo Balbi on his left. In the background to the right of the Rialto bridge is the Campanile of S. Bartolomeo and in the far distance perhaps the dome of SS. Giovanni e Paolo.

A more detailed watercolour of the same view (with minor differences in the composition) is in the National Gallery of Scotland (W. 1372). Turner may well have referred to pencil drawings made in 1819 (TB CLXXV-72, for instance) for a more precise record of the architecture.

56

From my Bedroom, Venice   1840?
Watercolour over pencil with touches of bodycolour; 197 × 282 mm
Inscribed *verso*, in pencil: *From my Bedroom, Venice*

TB CCCXVI-3

The drawings listed in the 1909 *Inventory* of the Bequest under TB CCCXVI number thirty-seven loose sheets; that is to say, they did not originally form one coherent sketchbook (unlike TB CCCXV), and may conceivably include watercolours made on either of Turner's last two visits to Venice. This sheet shows the campanile of S. Stefano on the left, that of S. Moisè in the centre and of St Mark's on the right, a very wide panorama but one which the eye could just encompass. As Turner notes, this was the view from his room, which must have been on the north side of the Hotel Europa. Two separate indications point to the conclusion that this watercolour should be dated 1840 rather than 1833, namely the absence of a second tower immediately beside that of S. Stefano – the campanile of Sant' Angelo, which was demolished in 1837 – and the presence of scaffolding on the campanile of St Mark's, which is documented as being in place in 1840 but not in 1833.

57

A distant view of the entrance to the Grand Canal
1840?

Watercolour on creamy-buff paper; 229 × 305 mm

TB CCCXVI-13

A sheet from a group of five studies which are on a creamy-buff, slightly coarse paper. Turner used coloured backgrounds to enhance his tonal range, as in plates 31–42, which are from a series on grey paper, also c.1840. In the present group, his aim seems to be above all with evoking atmospheric effects – the hazy light of early morning, or the rich glow of twilight – so that the broadly handled, almost schematised, treatment of architectural features is deliberately allusive.

58

S. Maria della Salute with the Traghetto S. Maria Zobenigo   1840?

Watercolour over pencil; 243 × 304 mm

TB CCCXVI-1

It is not easy to determine to what extent Turner's Venetian watercolours were made on the spot: sketchiness is not of itself much of an indication. The most likely signs are simplicity of design and colour and topographical truth. Here, Turner represents the buildings in their correct proportions and at the correct distance from the eye, without any capricious rearrangement. This study may have been used by Turner as reference for a more elaborately developed watercolour, which later belonged to Ruskin (Pl. 93).

59

S. Maria della Salute, the Campanile of St Mark's, the Ducal Palace and S. Giorgio Maggiore from the Giudecca   1840?

Watercolour over touches of pencil; 245 × 305 mm

TB CCCXVI-2

In colouring – the soft tones of salmon-pink and pale ochre – this sketch has similarities with those illustrated on plates 61 and 84, although this sheet has less pencil underdrawing and the sky is more elaborately worked. While plates 61 and 84 seem to have been drawn and possibly coloured on the spot, this watercolour has a degree of generalisation suggesting that it was drawn from memory. C.F. Bell, in his annotations to A.J. Finberg's *In Venice with Turner*, 1930, noted that the Campanile is shown with scaffolding in place: however, Turner's indications of form are here so indistinct that they are difficult to interpret accurately.

60

The Rialto, from the Riva del Carbon   after 1818

Watercolour over pencil; 181 × 267 mm

TB CCCXVI-7

Although this sheet was grouped by A.J. Finberg with the sketchbooks and watercolours he believed to be connected with Turner's later visits to Venice, it is in fact a tracing of a composition dating from shortly before he first went to the city in 1819. He had been commissioned to paint twenty watercolours of Italian views, based on drawings made on the spot in 1816–17 by James Hakewill (1788–1843), a minor topographical artist and writer. Hakewill had originally planned to publish his *Picturesque Tour of Italy* – essentially a middlebrow compilation of extracts from popular guidebooks – with engravings after his own drawings. However, presumably to broaden the appeal and thus increase sales of the work, he approached a number of well-known artists, including Turner, with the idea that they should work up his drawings into watercolours for engraving. Turner was paid 200 guineas in June 1818 by Hakewill's publisher John Murray for ten watercolours, contributing twenty in all, though only eighteen were in the event engraved. The publication was issued intermittently in parts and then, in the autumn of 1820, as a book. Financially, the publication was less than a success, and, perhaps to offset his losses on the project, Murray began to sell Turner's watercolours in 1824. The whereabouts of his original design for *The Rialto* (w. 700) is unknown, as also of another Venetian subject *The Custom House (Dogana) & Church of the Madonna della Salute, at the entrance of the Grand Canal*, which was never engraved.

This watercolour is a tracing either of the original watercolour or of John Pye's engraving, published in 1820 (the pencil outline is the same size as the engraving, fig. 1). It is difficult to know whether Turner made it simply as a record of the composition or because he intended to develop it further, perhaps as another watercolour; or to determine when he made the copy. If this is a tracing of the watercolour, it must date from before the original came into John Murray's possession. This view was to become a familiar motif in Turner's Venetian sketchbooks and watercolours, as well as the subject of a large unfinished painting (Tate Gallery, London).

61

On the Giudecca looking towards Fusina   1840?

Watercolour over pencil; 243 × 309 mm

Inscribed in pencil: *Redentore Ruintore* [?] *Capella S. Dominico*

TB CCCXVI-9

This sheet seems to have been drawn on the spot, although it is difficult to tell whether Turner added the delicate touches of colour at the same time or away from the motif: the pencil notes give the drawing the character of a page from one of the sketchbooks which he constantly used for rapid annotated studies. Turner's viewpoint was probably just in front of the Zitelle, looking towards the Redentore on the left and the church of the Gesuati on the right. His note *S. Dominico* must be a reference to this church: the order of the Poveri Gesuati merged with the Dominicans in 1668.

62

S. Maria della Salute, the Campanile and S. Giorgio Maggiore from the Canale della Grazia   1840?

Pencil and watercolour with touches of pen and red ink; 242 × 304 mm

TB CCCXVI-19

Turner's viewpoint here is not far away from that in plate 61 (see also Pl. 86, which is essentially the same composition as this), but the style, mood and intention of the two watercolours could hardly be more different. Instead of a rapid topographical notation, this is a carefully conceived exploration of colour relationships, in which cool turquoise tones are contrasted with warm topaz in two clearly defined areas. This sheet could well be among those that were worked up at a later date.

63

The Ducal Palace and the Riva degli Schiavoni   1840?

Watercolour with touches of white bodycolour, pen and red, brown and purple ink; 243 × 304 mm

Inscribed in pencil, illegibly, in Turner's hand

TB CCCXVI-17

This is among the most sumptuously coloured and densely worked of the Venetian watercolours in the Bequest, comparable in style with some of the sheets which Turner either gave away or sold. The illegible pencil inscription may (like similar notes made on some of his Swiss studies) suggest that this was a subject he intended to develop into a finished watercolour for sale to a particular patron. There are in fact no Venetian watercolours comparable in their final conception and execution with Turner's late Swiss series, which were worked up from studies of this type.

64

The Riva degli Schiavoni from the channel to the Lido 1840?

Watercolour and bodycolour with pen and brown and red ink;
245 × 305 mm

TB CCCXVI-18

The combination of cool tones of aquamarine merging into shades of
yellow with touches of pink was one which Turner frequently used in
his Venetian watercolours; a comparable sheet is illustrated in plate 62.
A network of fine pen lines is used to suggest the general forms of
buildings along the Riva degli Schiavoni, and to give definition to the
foreground detail of fishermen hauling in their nets.

65

The Riva degli Schiavoni, from near S. Biagio 1840?

Watercolour and bodycolour with pen and red and brown ink;
243 × 303 mm

Inscribed *verso*: *Beppo Club*

TB CCCXVI-21

Like several other sheets (for instance, those illustrated on Pls 64, 70)
grouped by A.J. Finberg in his *Inventory* of the Bequest under TB
CCCXVI, this is watermarked 1828. There is thus some argument for
dating them to Turner's second visit to Venice, made in 1833, but
stylistically they accord more closely with watercolours datable *c.*1840
and are therefore tentatively associated with his third and last visit to
the city made that year.

This watercolour shares similarities of composition and style with
that illustrated on plate 71 – also a view taken from the far end of the
Riva degli Schiavoni. Here, the foreground details of striped awnings
and a group of buildings to the right are emphasised with coarse
touches of pen and ink.

66

The Ducal Palace from the Dogana 1840?

Watercolour with pen and red ink over black chalk; 246 × 309 mm

TB CCCXVI-34

Turner's ability to develop a pictorial composition with colour and tone
rather than solid form is illustrated in this schematic watercolour: his
interest is in creating an effect of space through the juxtaposition of
washes of colour without relying on traditional procedures for drawing
perspective. Form is indicated only minimally by broad touches of
colour in the foreground to suggest boats moored in the Bacino, while
the buildings in the middle distance are indicated with the merest
flicker of pen and red ink.

67

Shipping off the Riva degli Schiavoni, from near the Ponte dell'Arsenale 1840?

Watercolour; 243 × 306 mm

TB CCCXVI-20

This is one of the Venetian studies in which Turner used a rather cooler
range of colours than usual and in which detail is indicated only very
summarily. While A.J. Finberg praised 'the colour of the water . . . an
ecstasy of the most heavenly blue', he went on to lament 'but it is only a
moment of rapture set in a ghostly confusion of shipping, palaces,
churches and towers'.

68

S. Giorgio Maggiore and S. Maria della Salute: calm at sunrise 1840?

Watercolour with pen and red ink; 222 × 325 mm

Coll.: John Ruskin, by whom presented to the Museum 1861

The Syndics of the Fitzwilliam Museum, Cambridge (591; W. 1361)

In 1861 John Ruskin presented twenty-five drawings by Turner to the Fitzwilliam, complementing his gift of forty-eight to the Ashmolean a few months earlier. Ruskin included all the Venetian sketches he ever owned in these gifts to the University collections, perhaps because, as A.J. Finberg suggested, he was increasingly dismayed at the 'modernising' developments in Venice, which he saw as vandalistic.

This watercolour, like the other Venetian subjects in the Fitzwilliam Museum, is probably datable *c*.1840, and compares in technique (notably the use of pen and red ink to accentuate form) with those from the roll sketchbook, TB CCCXV. Turner probably used a number of books of this type, which were subsequently broken up, and various sheets extracted for sale or for presentation to friends.

69

The Riva degli Schiavoni   1840?

Watercolour with pen and red and purple-brown ink; 217 × 318 mm

Coll.: John Ruskin, by whom presented to the Museum 1861

The Ashmolean Museum, Oxford (w. 1364)

Together with two other Venetian watercolours (Pls 91, 93), this was included in Ruskin's gift of forty-eight Turner drawings to the University of Oxford in 1861, shortly after he had completed *Modern Painters*. 'I've done my work about Turner as far as help was needed for it from drawings in my possession and I don't want to keep £1500 worth of him in my table drawers' (L. Herrmann, *Ruskin and Turner*, 1968, p. 31). The three Venetian watercolours are similar in size and type to the series in the Turner Bequest, and must have been extracted from sketchbooks of the type in which the sheets in TB CCCXV were originally bound. This watercolour and that of *The Accademia* (Pl. 91) would particularly have appealed to Ruskin's taste: plenty of detail, colourful, yet relatively clear and well-ordered compositions.

70

The approach to Venice: sunset   1840?

Watercolour and bodycolour over traces of pencil on off-white paper; 230 × 324 mm

TB CCCXVI-16

This is among the most lyrical of Turner's Venetian watercolours. It is developed to a degree comparable with some of the artist's Swiss 'specimen' drawings of the early 1840s, which were shown to patrons in order to give them some idea of what a finished design might look like, and it is conceivable that Turner intended to paint a number of Venetian watercolours for exhibition or for sale. In composition, this recalls one of Turner's earliest Venetian subjects, a view of the city from Fusina (in both drawings, the distant silhouette of the city is very similar), painted in 1821 for Walter Fawkes of Farnley Hall (w. 721). In a number of later watercolours, the subject is the same as in earlier years, but the mood is quite different. While the 1821 composition is bright, bustling with activity and essentially a straightforward topographical work, this watercolour is imbued with something of the same elegiac qualities that characterise the painting of the *Campo Santo* (Pl. 102), exhibited in 1842.

71

The Ponte della Pietà on the Riva degli Schiavoni
1840?

Watercolour over indications of black chalk; 244 × 305 mm

TB CCCXVI-30

Both this and the following watercolour show similar views across the Bacino di San Marco from points along the Riva degli Schiavoni; in the foreground is the Ponte della Pietà. From here Turner could look out to the Lagoon or back towards the crescent of buildings punctuated by the Campanile and, in the distance, the domes of the Salute. In this watercolour, his treatment of the light from the setting sun, reflected in the water, is particularly beautiful. The use of a vertical line connecting sky and sea combined with a receding diagonal – here the bridge – was a favourite compositional device of his (derived ultimately from Claude) in paintings and watercolours depicting absolutely calm weather.

72

The Ponte Ca'di Dio (?) 1840?

Watercolour with touches of white bodycolour over black chalk;
245 × 303 mm

TB CCCXVI-23

A view looking west towards the Ducal Palace and the Campanile of St Mark's, perhaps taken from near the Ponte Ca'di Dio at the eastern end of the Riva degli Schiavoni.

The foreground detail is emphasised not, as so often in the Venetian watercolours, with fine touches of pen and ink but with emphatic strokes of a brush charged with black wash. Similar handling can be seen in the watercolour illustrated on plate 46.

73

The Grand Canal, looking towards the Dogana
1840?

Watercolour and bodycolour with pen and red ink; 221 × 320 mm

Coll.: Hon. W.F.D. Smith; Sir Joseph Beecham sale Christie's 4 May 1917 (lot 156), bought Agnew; R.W. Lloyd, by whom bequeathed to the Museum 1958

The Trustees of the British Museum (1958-7-12-443; w. 1359)

Similar in viewpoint to plate 34, although Turner is on this occasion slightly nearer to the Dogana, and omits the Salute on the right of the composition. This vista looking down the Grand Canal had been a favourite of the artist's since his first visit of 1819 (TB CLXXV-67 *verso* is a pencil sketch taken from almost the same spot). Stylistically, this watercolour accords with others of the early 1840s, especially in the use of pen and red ink to suggest detail.

Although the great majority of Turner's Venetian watercolours form part of the artist's Bequest, a number of sheets seem to have been given away or sold (perhaps through his agent Thomas Griffith) during his lifetime. These are more highly worked than those in the Bequest, and doubtless accorded more closely with contemporary taste.

74

View from the roof of the Hotel Europa
1833 or 1840?

Watercolour over black chalk with touches of white; 246 × 305 mm

TB CCCXVI-36

The dating of this watercolour is problematic. If it is related to the composition of *Juliet and her Nurse* (Pl. 97), it must pre-date 1836. The connection may, however, simply be coincidental, and it has been suggested that (like the majority of the loose sheets grouped together under TB CCCXVI) it should be dated 1840 or later; other comparable views from an upper window or the roof of the Europa include TB CCCLXIV-43, TB CCCXVI-5, 42, and plate 56, which can be dated 1840 on topographical evidence. Nevertheless, so evocative is this sheet of the key foreground detail in *Juliet and her Nurse* that it is tempting to associate the two, even though the view over the Piazza in the painting is clearly different.

75

The Arsenal 1840?

Watercolour and bodycolour; 243 × 308 mm

Verso: pencil studies of carts, horses and figures

TB CCCXVI-27

This is one of the most striking and brilliantly coloured of Turner's Venetian studies. In choosing a low viewpoint and almost thrusting the spectator into the composition Turner may have had in mind the dramatic architectural prints of Piranesi, which he had admired since his youth.

The Arsenal (which gave its name, from the Arabic *Dar sina'a*, meaning 'House of Construction', to all subsequent dockyards and munitions stores) had been the source of Venice's maritime power and wealth, for without her fleet she would have been nothing. At the height of the city's prosperity Dante noted that the Arsenal employed 16,000 workmen; by 1822, according to Byron's friend John Cam Hobhouse, there were only 250.

76

S. Giorgio Maggiore (?)   1840?

Watercolour; 225 × 290 mm

Coll.: Henry Vaughan, by whom bequeathed to the Gallery 1900

National Gallery of Ireland, Dublin (2417; W. 1357)

Although described as a view of S. Giorgio Maggiore, the relationship of the campanile to the church, and the silhouette of the roof line, suggests that this must be a church on one of the islands in the Lagoon.

77

S. Giorgio Maggiore at sunset from the Hotel Europa   1840?

Watercolour; 244 × 306 mm

TB CCCXVI-24

A number of Turner's Venetian watercolours seem to anticipate the studies he was to make in Switzerland in the early 1840s, notably those of the Rigi (the distinctively shaped mountain facing Lucerne across the lake), which he drew in all lights and weather conditions, recording its changing appearance in an extraordinary sequence of colour harmonies. The view across the Bacino to S. Giorgio Maggiore offered Turner similar inspiration and his studies of the church in its watery setting range from delicate washes of translucent colour to the richest tones of sunset (see, for example, Pls 78, 84). The degree of detail with which he renders architectural forms also varies: here he has discarded all inessentials in the interest of light and colour.

78

S. Giorgio Maggiore from the Dogana   1840?

Watercolour and bodycolour over pencil; 193 × 281 mm

TB CCCXVI-28

A more detailed view of S. Giorgio than the preceding watercolour, this also shows the church at sunset, and is among the most brilliant of Turner's Venetian studies of reflected light and colour. Henry James was to describe the 'suffusion of rosiness' in the buildings of S. Giorgio, an effect which this study perfectly expresses.

79

The Lagoon, behind S. Giorgio Maggiore (?) 1840?

Watercolour and bodycolour; 245 × 305 mm

TB CCCXVI-31

Described by C.F. Bell in his annotations to A.J. Finberg's *In Venice with Turner*, 1930, as 'an imaginative fantasy', the topographical element in this watercolour is of minor importance. Turner's interest here is in the numerous small boats in the Bacino, which were still such a striking feature of the Venetian waterfront at this date. The summary yet expressive treatment of the boats, the brilliance of the blue-green water and the blaze of clear light are the most striking features of this sheet.

80

The Grand Canal   1840?

Watercolour; 218 × 319 mm

Coll.: Henry Vaughan, by whom bequeathed to the Gallery 1900

National Gallery of Ireland, Dublin (2426; W. 1358)

In subject, mood and style this watercolour may be grouped with those illustrated on plates 86–89, which show the city and the Lagoon under threatening storm clouds. This sheet was probably worked up after Turner's return to England, to judge by the somewhat generalised and capricious treatment of topography: the buildings at the entrance to the Grand Canal and along the Molo have taken on a cliff-like appearance.

81

Moonlight   1840?

Watercolour with touches of bodycolour; 245 × 303 mm

TB CCCXVI-39

As well as the series of studies on brown paper which included scenes of firework displays and mysterious glimpses of the city by night (see Pls 10, 15, 28, 29), Turner also made a few watercolours on white paper of moonlit views on the Lagoon. This sheet is a particularly subtle and velvety example, using a limited range of colours, chiefly blues and blacks, against which tiny glimmers of light from the boats sparkle against the darkness.

82

St Mark's and the Ducal Palace   1840?

Watercolour with touches of bodycolour; 247 × 307 mm

TB CCCXVI-35

The central area of the composition is suggested only very schematic-ally, a broad wash of aquamarine for the water, touches of pale ochre and grey to represent the buildings, and accents of red on the Campanile and on the boats in the foreground.

83

Venice from Fusina (?)   1840?

Watercolour; 241 × 302 mm

Verso: An indecipherable inscription – perhaps a quotation – in Turner's hand which seems to refer to the setting sun

TB CCCXVI-25

This study was among the 'First Hundred' drawings selected by Ruskin for public exhibition; it is justly among the most famous of Turner's Venetian watercolours. Ruskin suggested that the inspiration for it may have come to Turner while returning to Venice from Torcello, in which case he would have been facing west, towards the sunset. A.J. Finberg, however, listed it in the *Inventory* as Venice from Fusina, in which case it would be a study of sunrise. Turner's inscription on the *verso* tends to confirm Ruskin's description.

Ruskin wrote of this watercolour: 'The clouds are remarkable as an example of Turner's frequent practice of laying rich colour on a wet ground, and leaving it to graduate itself as it dried, a few subsequent touches being, in the present instance, added on the right hand. Although the boat in the centre seems a mere scrawl, the action of the gondolier . . . is perfectly given in his forward thrust.'

84

S. Giorgio Maggiore and the Zitelle from the Giudecca   1840?

Watercolour over pencil; 244 × 309 mm

TB CCCXVI-40

A drawing similar in character to that illustrated on plate 61, perhaps even sketched on the same day: the viewpoint for both studies is mid-way between the Zitelle and the Redentore, either somewhere along the Fondamenta, or from a boat moored nearby. In plate 61 he was looking to the left, up the Giudecca Canal towards Fusina, while here he was facing to the right. The sparing touches of watercolour (chiefly pink and orange, with accents of black for the boats) suggest that these drawings may also have been coloured on the spot.

85

Looking eastward towards the Campanile of St Mark's: sunrise? 1840?

Watercolour; 198 × 280 mm

TB CCCLXIV-106

Perhaps because this sheet became separated from the majority of the Venetian studies in the Bequest and was inventoried under the heading 'miscellaneous' it is among the less well known watercolours of Venice. It can be probably dated 1840 or soon afterwards: other studies of the same kind no doubt remain to be identified in the Bequest. Some of Turner's most evocative watercolours are of sunrise or sunset skies, and here he uses one of his most dramatic colour combinations: an intense violet, set off with lilac and pale yellow and touches of orange and scarlet. The foreground is summarily sketched, so that the emphasis is on the sky which dominates the composition. It is difficult – and not really of much importance – to determine the buildings which Turner has included, but he seems to be looking towards the Campanile of St Mark's, with the Ducal Palace in the centre and possibly the cupola of S. Giorgio Maggiore on the right.

Many of Turner's watercolours consist simply of broad washes or streaks of transparent colour brushed on to the paper. In their minimal indication of form they have no real precedent, nor any close parallel in the art of other watercolourists of his time, and reflect his continuous artistic experimentation. But they are never purely abstract, for there is always a foundation of the two phenomena in nature that preoccupied him throughout his career: water and sky. As in this example, some have a topographical basis, but represent not so much direct observation as a recreation from memory of effects of colour and tone. The apparently incomplete state and vagueness of studies of this kind, and the inexplicitness of the subject matter, caused A.J. Finberg to refer to them as 'Colour Beginnings', but they are gradually being placed more accurately in Turner's *oeuvre*.

86

A storm at sunset 1840?

Watercolour and bodycolour with scratching-out and touches of pen; 222 × 320 mm

Inscribed *verso* with eight lines of illegible verse

Coll.: John Ruskin, by whom presented to the Museum 1861

The Syndics of the Fitzwilliam Museum, Cambridge (590; W. 1353)

One of a number of stormy views of Venice which can probably be dated *c*.1840 or shortly afterwards; perhaps because of their particularly dramatic nature, they became separated from the main concentration of Venetian drawings and watercolours in the Bequest, presumably through Turner's agent in the 1840s, Thomas Griffith. Drawings from the group (W. 1352–5, 1358, 1371) have been associated with Turner's 1833 visit to Venice, but his patrons in the early 1840s would probably have wanted to acquire examples of his most recent work. This watercolour is in fact on paper watermarked 1834 (as is the roll sketchbook, TB CCCXV), suggesting that it was painted either some time after his second visit, or, as seems more likely, *c*.1840. Stylistically also most of them are closer in style to those Venetian watercolours generally accepted as dating from his third and last visit in 1840.

87

A storm on the Lagoon 1840?

Watercolour with pen and bodycolour; 218 × 318 mm

Coll.: William Quilter, sale Christie's 8 April 1878 (lot 240), bought Agnew; Rev. C.J. Sale, by whom bequeathed to the Museum 1915

The Trustees of the British Museum (1915-3-13-50; W. 1354)

The most atmospheric of the group of storm scenes (see Pls 86, 88) this is also more fully resolved than the majority of Turner's Venetian watercolours. Unlike plate 86, this sheet is not watermarked with a date, but the stylistic evidence, in particular the treatment of the architecture on the left, tends to suggest a date of 1840 or later. Turner's virtuosity in depicting the menacing sky, the drift of misty rain on the left, through which a campanile (indicated simply by dragging a brush through the wet paint) looms out, and the churning sea, is extraordinarily powerful. Clarkson Stanfield's attempt at a similar subject, plate 109, seems puny by comparison.

The gondola dominates the foreground, and in this instance, perhaps more than in any other of Turner's Venetian subjects, provides a visual parallel to Shelley's eerie description: 'The gondolas . . . are things of a most romantic and picturesque appearance; I can only compare them to moths of which a coffin might have been the chrysalis' (*Letters*, ed. F.L. Jones, 1964, vol. II, p. 42).

88

A storm in the Piazzetta   1840?

Watercolour, bodycolour, pen and ink and scratching-out; 221 × 321 mm

Coll.: Henry Vaughan, by whom bequeathed to the Gallery 1900

National Galleries of Scotland, Edinburgh (D(NG) 871; W. 1352)

The dense colouring of this watercolour – almost as if painted on a coloured ground – is a little reminiscent of the series of studies on brown paper (especially those showing fireworks) which were perhaps made by Turner in 1833. However, this sheet is watermarked 1834 and must therefore post-date that visit. The dramatic light effects are achieved not by touches of white bodycolour, as in plates 28 and 29, but by scratching and rubbing through the pigment into the white paper.

89

Venice from the Lagoon   1840?

Watercolour, bodycolour, pen and ink and scraping-out; 222 × 320 mm

Coll.: Henry Vaughan by whom bequeathed to the Gallery 1900

National Galleries of Scotland, Edinburgh (D(NG) 872; W. 1371)

This sheet is watermarked 1834, thus post-dating Turner's 1833 visit to Venice. Either it was painted in England after his return from Italy or it is related to his last visit in 1840. The dramatic motif of the steamship moving across the Lagoon, its plume of black smoke billowing into the sky, appealed to Turner who included steamships in several pictures, notably in *The Fighting 'Temeraire'*, 1839 (The National Gallery, London). Turner relished such dramatic contrasts between past and present, and as C.R. Leslie noted, he had 'an almost prophetic idea of smoke, soot, iron and steam, coming to the front in all naval matters'. Ruskin expressed himself very differently, writing to his father in September 1845, 'How painful it is to be in Venice now . . . There is no single spot . . . where her spirit remains; the modern work has set its plague spot everywhere; the moment you begin to *feel*, some gaspipe business forces itself on the eye and you are thrust with the 19th century, until you dream, as Mr Harding [James Duffield Harding 1798–1863, artist] did last night, that your very gondola has become a steamer.' During a later visit to Italy, he complained about 'the accursed whistling of the dirty steam-engine of the omnibus for the Lido, waiting at the Quay of the Ducal Palace for the dirty population of Venice . . . [which] smokes and spits up and down the piazzetta all day, and gets itself dragged by a screaming kettle to Lido next morning' (*Works*, XXVII, p. 328).

90

The Piazzetta and the Ducal Palace   1840?

Watercolour; 240 × 304 mm

Coll.: Henry Vaughan, by whom bequeathed to the Gallery 1900

National Gallery of Ireland, Dublin (2423; W. 1356)

Like those other Venetian watercolours that seem to have been given away or sold during Turner's lifetime, this is a comparatively highly finished example, probably painted shortly after his return from Venice in 1840. Although there are differences of style, this sheet complements the *Storm in the Piazzetta* (Pl. 88), which was also owned by Henry Vaughan. Here the Piazzetta is seen from the opposite direction, as if from a boat moored in the Bacino.

91

The Accademia 1840?

Watercolour over slight pencil indications, with pen and red and black ink and some scraping-out; 217 × 318 mm

Coll.: John Ruskin, by whom presented to the Museum 1861

The Ashmolean Museum, Oxford (W. 1366)

In his *Guide to the Principal Pictures in the Academy of Fine Arts at Venice*, 1877, Ruskin included a description of the exterior of the Accademia, which he wrote 'if any of my readers care for either Turner or me, they should look at with some moments' pause; for I have given Turner's lovely sketch of it to Oxford, painted as he saw it fifty years ago, with bright golden sails grouped in front of it where now is the ghastly iron bridge'. Until 1854 the Grand Canal had been spanned only at the Rialto, and the iron bridge was apparently constructed to enable the Austrian military governor to deploy troops more rapidly for the quelling of possible disorders. The present wooden bridge, originally intended only as a temporary construction, replaced it in 1932. The Accademia was established in its present buildings (the former convent of the Carità) in 1807 on the initiative of the French. At the same time the neo-classical entrance façade was erected; this is seen to the right of centre in Turner's watercolour.

92

S. Maria della Salute, from the Canal 1840?

Watercolour and bodycolour with pen and brown ink; 222 × 322 mm

Coll.: Henry Vaughan, by whom bequeathed to the Gallery 1900

National Galleries of Scotland, Edinburgh (D(NG) 888; W. 1370)

Very few of Turner's Venetian watercolours, apart from the series of studies on brown paper (see Pls 24, 25, 30), concentrate on single buildings or architectural features: the nearest comparable sheet to this is a view of the Arsenal (Pl. 75), which shares similarities of composition. In this study of the west side of the Salute, Turner includes sufficient detail to suggest the façade of the church and then irradiates the composition in a haze of golden light.

93

The Grand Canal, looking towards S. Maria della Salute 1840?

Watercolour over pencil, with pen and red and blue ink, heightened with touches of white bodycolour; 215 × 315 mm

Coll.: John Ruskin, by whom presented to the Museum 1861

The Ashmolean Museum, Oxford (W. 1363)

Of the three Venetian watercolours presented by Ruskin to Oxford in 1861 (see Pls 69, 91), this is perhaps the most beautiful, wonderfully atmospheric in mood, pure and delicate in execution. The palazzi on the left are drawn with fine pen lines of scarlet and blue, and reflected in the waters of the Canal in tones of violet, blue and pink, while the Salute and Dogana are in shades of blue, and a very pale wash of yellow can be seen in the sky, water and buildings along the Riva degli Schiavoni. The view is taken from one of Turner's favourite vantage points, in mid-stream near the spot where the Accademia Bridge was to be erected in 1854 (see Pl. 91).

94

The Grand Canal with S. Maria della Salute
c.1840

Watercolour with bodycolour and scraping-out over traces of pencil; 218 × 318 mm

Coll.: Thomas Griffith; by descent to the present owner

Private Collection (W. 1368)

One of the most highly developed of Turner's Venetian subjects, this may have been intended as a study for sale, or for presentation to a client as a sample of a fully elaborated composition. It is possible that it was painted some time after Turner's return to England. The sheet belonged to the artist's agent Thomas Griffith, perhaps given to him in acknowledgement of his services – he was the intermediary in Turner's project of the 1840s to paint a series of Swiss watercolours on commission for various patrons, based on studies of a comparable kind – or lent to him to show clients and never returned.

95

The Sun of Venice   1840?

Watercolour with pen; 219 × 317 mm

Coll.: Henry Vaughan, by whom bequeathed to the Gallery 1900

National Galleries of Scotland, Edinburgh (D(NG) 875; W. 1374)

This drawing takes its title from the emblem painted on the sail of the fishing boat at the left. Although it is not an exact study for the painting of the same subject exhibited in 1843 (Pl. 103) – Turner rarely made direct preparatory studies in watercolour for his works in oil – he may well have had this sheet by him when working on the painting. His interest in sketching similar small craft while in Venice is shown by numerous rapid pencil sketches in TB CCCXIV. Such assimilation of detail particularly impressed the young Ruskin, who wrote home to his father in September 1845: 'I *was* a little taken aback when yesterday, at six in the morning, with the early sunlight just flushing its folds, out came a fishing boat with its *painted* sail full to the wind, the most gorgeous orange and red, in everything, form, colour, & feeling, the very counterpart of the Sol di Venezia.'

96

Bridge of Sighs, Ducal Palace and Custom-House, Venice: Canaletti painting   1833

Oil on mahogany; 51 × 82.5 cm

Coll.: Robert Vernon, purchased at the R.A. 1833 for 200 guineas and given to the National Gallery 1847; transferred to the Tate Gallery 1912

Exh.: R.A. 1833, no. 109

The Tate Gallery, London (370; B/J 349)

Turner did not exhibit any oil paintings of Venice until 1833 (fourteen years after his first visit to the city), when he showed this picture and the now lost *Ducal Palace, Venice*. Venetian subjects, however, were subsequently to form a significant proportion of his exhibited works. It has been suggested that Turner's revival of interest in the city may have been prompted by a second visit in 1832, but all the available evidence suggests that he did not return to Venice until the late summer of 1833, after the closing of the Royal Academy exhibition.

As the title suggests, Turner was paying homage to that most celebrated painter of Venice, Canaletto, who is shown on the left, improbably working at a picture which Turner shows in an elaborate gilt frame. The fact that Canaletto almost certainly never painted out-of-doors is, in Turner's context, irrelevant. His intention, as with other paintings in which he included the presence of artists whom he greatly admired – *Raphael in Rome from the Vatican*, exh. 1820 or *Watteau Study by Fresnoy's rule*, exh. 1831, for instance, was partly autobiographical: he was identifying himself with the great artistic traditions of the past.

However, the immediate stimulus for this painting seems to have been a sense of good-natured rivalry with Clarkson Stanfield (see fig. 7), who had already established a reputation for his Venetian subjects. According to a contemporary account, on hearing that Stanfield was painting a similar view, Turner determined 'to give him a lesson in atmosphere and poetry'. To judge from reviews of the exhibition it was generally thought that Turner had triumphed : 'Stanfield's exhibit is to Turner's picture what a mere talent is to genius' (*The Spectator*, 11 May 1833), 'the juxtaposition brought out more glaringly the defects of Stanfield, and illustrated more strongly the fine powers of Turner . . . [it] displayed a brilliancy, breadth and power, killing every other work in the exhibition' (*Arnold's Magazine*, iii, 1833–4, pp. 408–9). For the critic of another periodical, it was 'more his own than he seems aware of: he imagines he has painted it in the Canaletto style: the style is his, and worth Canaletti's ten times over' (*The Athenaeum*, 11 May 1833).

By comparison with his next Venetian subject, exhibited in 1834, *Venice* (National Gallery of Art, Washington D.C.), this painting has a somewhat stilted, unatmospheric quality, which tends to confirm the idea that he painted it before revisiting the city.

97

Juliet and her Nurse   1836

Oil on canvas; 92 × 123 cm

Coll.: Bought by H.A.J. Munro of Novar at the R.A. exhibition in 1836; Munro sale, Christie's 6 April 1878 (lot 100) bought by Agnew; Kirkman Hodgson M.P. from whom bought by Agnew in 1893 and sold to James Price; Messrs Wallis 1895; Colonel O.H. Payne, New York by 1901; his nephew, Harry Payne Whitney 1917; his widow Gertrude Vanderbilt Whitney 1930; her daughter Mrs Flora Whitney Miller; sold Sotheby Parke Bernet, New York, 29 May 1980 (lot 44) bought by the present owner.

Exh.: R.A. 1836, no. 73

Sra Amalia Lacroze de Fortabat, Argentina (B/J 365)

This is arguably the greatest of Turner's Venetian paintings. When it was first exhibited at the Royal Academy in 1836, however, it was the subject of fierce attack in *Blackwood's Magazine* by the Rev. John Eagles, an amateur artist and conventionally-minded critic, who was persistently hostile to Turner. Eagles described the picture as 'A strange jumble – "confusion worse confounded" . . . Amidst so many absurdities, we scarcely stop to ask why Juliet and her nurse should be at Venice.' It was this attack that led the seventeen-year-old Ruskin to draft a reply, which, however, was never printed in his lifetime as Turner, to whom he sent it, advised against publication ('I never move in these matters. They are of no import save mischief'). This precociously brilliant essay contained the germ of *Modern Painters*. So far from being fanciful, gaudy and careless, as had been claimed by his critics, Turner's paintings were founded strictly on natural observation, although they were not prosaically naturalistic, and were dazzling in colouring and masterly in handling. His imagination, Ruskin added, was 'Shakespearian in its mightiness'. In a dazzling evocation of the painting he wrote: 'Many-coloured mists are floating above the distant city, but such mists as you might imagine to be aetherial spirits . . . wandering in vague and infinite glory around the earth they have loved . . . they move and mingle among the pale stars, and rise up into the brightness of the illimitable heaven, whose soft, sad blue eye gazes down into the deep waters of the sea for ever . . . And the spires of the glorious city rise indistinctly bright into those living mists like the pyramids of pale fire from some vast altar [an image perhaps derived from Shelley's *Lines Written among the Euganean Hills*, lines

105–14] . . . This picture can be, and ought only to be viewed as embodied enchantment, delineated magic . . . Turner is an exception to all rules, and can be judged by no standard of art' (*Works*, vol. III, pp. 635–40).

In his decision to set a scene from *Romeo and Juliet* in Venice, Turner was obviously influenced by the romantic atmosphere of the city – perhaps also by its underlying mood of melancholy that similarly haunts Shakespeare's play. It has recently been suggested that the Juliet of the title was not Shakespeare's heroine but the 'lovely Giulietta' of Samuel Rogers's poem *Italy*, published in 1830 (which Turner had helped to illustrate, see Pl. 6), the fiancée of a young Venetian, Marcolini, who was executed in the Piazza of St Mark's for a murder he never committed, but this argument has been convincingly refuted (Butlin and Joll, revised edition, 1984, pp. 216–17). Perhaps influenced by criticism of the incongruity, Turner dropped the Shakespearean association from the title when the picture was engraved in 1842. It was now called *St Mark's Place, Venice (Moonlight)* and accompanied by four lines beginning '. . . but Beauty doth not die' adapted from *Childe Harold's Pilgrimage* (quoted in the Introduction, see p. 9). Turner was less concerned with the apparent subject than with – as Ruskin appreciated – establishing a mood. His sources, literary, historical or classical, were simply the starting point from which his visual imagination could soar, untrammelled by literal dependence on his subject.

98

Venice, the Piazzetta with the Ceremony of the Doge marrying the Sea   *c.*1835

Oil on canvas; 91.5 × 122 cm

Coll.: Turner Bequest 1856; transferred to the Tate Gallery 1948

The Tate Gallery, London (4446; B/J 501)

An unfinished painting from the Turner Bequest, which the artist seems to have abandoned at a comparatively advanced stage; it has been dated *c.*1835 because of its technique which accords with other works of the mid-1830s. Formerly given a straightforward topographical title, it has more recently been suggested that Turner intended to depict the ceremony held annually until 1797 on Ascension Day, when the Doge was rowed on the Bucintoro from the Molo to the mouth of the Lido, where he cast a ring into the sea to symbolise both Venice's supremacy over and dependence on the Adriatic. Turner would have been familiar with seventeenth- and eighteenth-century depictions of the event, which, with its splendid ceremonial, was a favourite subject, most notably with Canaletto, whose painting (Pl. 106) shows the same scene as Turner's – the embarkation of the Doge. Characteristically, however, Turner seems to have condensed into one episode the departure from the Molo with the actual ceremony.

99

Venice, the Bridge of Sighs   1840

Oil on canvas; 61 × 91.5 cm

Coll.: Turner Bequest 1856; transferred to the Tate Gallery 1961

Exh.: R.A. 1840, no. 55

The Tate Gallery, London (527; B/J 383)

One of two Venetian subjects exhibited by Turner at the Royal Academy in 1840 (see Pl. 100), this painting was almost ignored by reviewers, although it was included in *The Spectator's* sweeping denunciation of the artist's 'freaks of chromomania' (16 May 1840). A couplet based on lines from Byron's *Childe Harold's Pilgrimage* was included in the catalogue:

> I stood upon a bridge, a palace and
> A prison on each hand. – Byron

For Turner the beauty of the city concealed more sinister facts, and, like Byron, he seems to have been suggesting that Venice's past glories had depended on a despotic and inherently corrupt system of government.

100

Venice, from the Canale della Giudecca, Chiesa di S. Maria della Salute, &c.   1840

Oil on canvas; 61 × 91.4 cm

Coll.: Painted for John Sheepshanks who gave his collection to the Government in 1856

Exh.: R.A. 1840, no. 71

Victoria and Albert Museum, London (B/J 384)

So startled were most of the critics by Turner's chief exhibits at the Royal Academy in 1840 – notably *The Slave Ship* (Museum of Fine Arts, Boston), *The New Moon* (Tate Gallery, London) and *Rockets and Blue Lights* (Sterling and Francine Clark Art Institute, Williamstown) – *The Spectator* describing them as 'flaring abortions' and as 'the rhapsodies of Turner's insane pencil', that his two Venetian subjects (see Pl. 99) were almost overlooked. This painting was specifically noted only in *Blackwood's Magazine*, where it was damned with faint praise: 'Turner again! Is there anything to enable us to put in a good word? There is. The sky is very natural, and has its due aerial perspective; all the rest is wretched: buildings as if built of snow by children in sport.'

As Butlin and Joll note, the painting is in an exceptionally good state of preservation, so that even today S. Maria della Salute looks as strikingly white as it did to the artist's contemporaries. It is said that this is due to the fact that in 1893 the painting was sealed *in vacuo* in a specially designed case, in which it has subsequently remained. Ruskin, however, always one to be pessimistic about the physical deterioration of Turner's work, believed that his paintings were generally most vulnerable during the first year or so after their execution.

Turner began work on the picture at the end of January 1840, when he wrote to John Sheepshanks enquiring the size he wished it to be. Sheepshanks, a prosperous clothier, characteristic of the successful middle-class patrons who became Turner's most loyal clients in the 1830s and 1840s, had built up a notable collection of Dutch and Flemish prints, which he sold to the British Museum in 1836 and, with the proceeds, began to collect contemporary British art. This collection, including five oil paintings by Turner, was presented to the government in 1856 and is now in the Victoria and Albert Museum.

101

The Dogano, San Giorgio, Citella, from the Steps of the Europa   1842

Oil on canvas; 62 × 92.5 cm

Coll.: Robert Vernon, purchased at the R.A. 1842, and given to the National Gallery 1847; transferred to the Tate Gallery 1949

Exh.: R.A. 1842, no. 52

The Tate Gallery, London (372; B/J 396)

Exhibited at the Royal Academy in the same year as the *Campo Santo* (Pl. 102), contemporary critics generally treated the two as a pair, praising them as 'among the loveliest, because least exaggerated pictures, which this magician (for such he is, in right of his command over the spirits of Air, Fire, and Water) has recently given us. Fairer dreams never floated past poets' eye; and the aspect of the city of Waters is hardly one iota idealised' (*The Athenaeum*, 7 May 1842). Turner himself, however, seems to have intended more than was generally understood. The two paintings may be interpreted as a contrast between the grandeur and magnificence of the city represented in this picture, and the suggestion of death and decay symbolised by the cemetery of the Campo Santo. Here the supremacy of Venice as a great trading city is alluded to by showing the Dogana (customs house) which is surmounted by the figure of Fortune. John Gage (in Ruskinian mood) has recently drawn attention to a curious detail in the right foreground, where two exotically coloured oriental jars are shown on the lower step, perhaps representing the type of luxury goods imported to Europe by Venetian traders: though more durable, in the end they are no less illustrative of the eventual decline of Venice than the pieces of rubbish floating in the foreground of the *Campo Santo*. Such connotations of luxury and decay occur in several of the Venetian paintings of the early 1840s. He has also suggested that the group formed by the jars and the black and white dogs illustrates Turner's palette, with its contrasts of warm and cold tones, and extremes of light and shade.

Turner made many drawings and watercolours from the Hotel Europa, where he stayed during his later visits to Venice. This painting, unusually among his late works, seems to have been based on a pencil drawing in a sketchbook dating from his first visit to the city in 1819 (TB CLXXV-40). However, this was to become such a familiar viewpoint to Turner that the resemblance may simply be coincidental.

The painting was bought by Robert Vernon (who also owned Pl. 96). Between 1820 and 1847 he built up a collection of some 200 contemporary British pictures, most of which he presented to the National Gallery in 1847; this was the first painting by Turner to be exhibited in the National Gallery.

102

Campo Santo, Venice   1842

Oil on canvas; 62.2 × 92.7 cm

Coll.: Bought at the R.A. exhibition in 1842 by Elhanan Bicknell (or possibly painted on commission for him); Christie's 25 April 1863 (lot 112) bought Agnew for Henry McConnell; Christie's 27 March 1886 (lot 76) bought S. White for Mrs J.M. Keiller of Dundee; Edward Drummond Libbey 1916, by whom presented to the Toledo Museum 1926.

Exh.: R.A. 1842, no. 73

The Toledo Museum of Art, Toledo, Ohio (B/J 397)

In some ways the most exquisite of Turner's Venetian paintings, both in style and mood, this was exhibited at the Royal Academy in the same year as the preceding picture (Pl. 101); most critics treated the two as a pair, although they were immediately acquired by different owners. Turner himself may have thought of the two paintings as commentaries on the city's history, the cemetery of the Campo Santo symbolising the end of Venice's great imperial past. However, this theory is rendered somewhat less likely by the fact that the cemetery on the Island of S. Michele was of very recent construction, having been established on the site of a monastery suppressed during the French occupation and only brought into use in 1837. The now familiar straight brick walls, shown in Turner's painting, were built at that time. The cemetery was thus perhaps too new to have acquired the aura of a symbol, save in the most general sense. Certainly his choice of image struck Ruskin: as he wrote to his father from Venice in December 1851, 'I was thinking of adding to that passage about the cemetery . . . saying that Turner had been struck with it – and had made its long purple wall the subject of the second most lovely picture he ever painted of Venice.' It was probably this painting (although not specifically identified) that inspired one of Ruskin's most consciously poetic passages in the first edition of *Modern Painters* I, 1843 (omitted from subsequent editions), which reveals more fully than any other of Ruskin's writings the effect on him as a young man of Turner's vision of Venice (see p. 80).

103

The Sun of Venice going to sea 1843

Oil on canvas; 61.5 × 92 cm

Inscribed on sail: *Sol de VENEZA MI RAI.I . . .*

Coll.: Turner Bequest 1856; transferred to the Tate Gallery 1954

Exh.: R.A. 1843, no. 129

The Tate Gallery, London (535; B/J 402)

For Turner, this painting was intended to express something of the pessimism he had come to feel about Venice. The catalogue for the Royal Academy exhibition of 1843 included an extract from Turner's own fragmentary epic poem, *Fallacies of Hope*:

> Fair shines the morn, and soft the zephyrs blow
> Venezia's fisher spreads his painted sail so gay,
> Nor heeds the demon that in grim repose
> Expects his evening prey.

The imagery of these lines echoes a passage about Venice from Shelley's *Lines Written Among the Euganean Hills*:

> Sun-girt city, thou has been
> Ocean's child, and then his queen;
> Now is come a darker day,
> And thou soon must be his prey . . .
> The fisher on his watery way . . .
> Will spread his sail and seize his oar
> Till he pass the gloomy shore,
> Lest the dead should, from their sleep,
> Lead a rapid dance of death
> O'er the waters of his path.

Venice had come to have an emotional significance for Turner comparable to that of Carthage in earlier years; he was haunted by the 'fate of empire' and saw in the history of both cities a warning of the destiny that might one day overtake his own country. On another level,

he might also have been anticipating his own death, as the 'evening prey' of the grim demon.

The critics of the day apparently failed to understand Turner's pessimistic intention. Even Ruskin – for whom this was a favourite picture – seems to have ignored such connotations, emphasising instead Turner's mastery of transient natural phenomena. In a passage written for the third edition of *Modern Painters* I, published in 1846, after his return from a visit to Venice, where he had been struck by Turner's truth to nature (see Pl. 95), he praised 'the particular power of the picture [in] the painting of the sea surface . . . A stream of splendid colour fell from the boat . . . on each side a large space of water reflecting nothing but the morning sky. This was divided by an eddying swell, on whose continuous sides the local colour of the water was seen, pure aquamarine (a beautiful occurrence of closely observed truth); but still there remained a large blank space of pale water to be treated . . . there the water lay, no dead grey flat paint, but downright clear, playing, palpable surface, full of indefinite hue, and retiring as regularly and visibly back and far away . . . it is his having done this which made me say that "no man had ever painted the surface of calm water but Turner".'

104

Venice, Evening, going to the Ball 1845

Oil on canvas; 61.5 × 92.5 cm

Coll.: William Wethered, junior, of King's Lynn, Norfolk; apparently returned to Turner before the artist's death; Turner Bequest 1856; transferred to the Tate Gallery 1921

Exh.: R.A. 1845, no. 117

The Tate Gallery, London (543; B/J 416)

Turner exhibited four Venetian subjects at the Royal Academy in 1845; these were described as representing the 'effects of morning and evening, noon and sunset'. *The Spectator* praised the first two (of which this is the second, representing evening) for 'their magical effects of light and colour: the watery floor and aerial sky meet at the horizon in a gorgeous mass of orange and golden tints'. Sadly, the condition of the painting has deteriorated so that it is difficult to recognise the 'play of brilliant colours, sparkling as they vanish above smooth waters', described by another critic. 'The rising moon ... with its long gleam of light coming across the waters, is really a curiosity worthy of study. Stuck on with the palette knife, or the thumb, who would think it would give the soft, cool light it does,' commented the *Morning Chronicle* (17 May).

The titles of this painting and its pendant, *Returning from the Ball*, perhaps refer to a Venetian *Festa*, a subject which would surely have appealed to Turner. A second pair of paintings with the same titles was exhibited at the Academy in 1846 (the early histories of the 1845 and 1846 pictures have become tortuously confused – see Butlin and Joll, rev. ed., 1984, nos 416, 417, 421, 422), one of which seems to have been intended as a reminiscence of the Festa Santa Marta which was concerned with sole-fishing and included gaily lit decorated boats. In 1849, Chateaubriand, recalling a gondola procession for a Festa on the Lido, rhapsodied in a verbal equivalent of some of Turner's paintings '*J'avais une autre raison d'aller au Lido, à savoir mon envie de dire un mot de tendresse à la mer, ma mignonne, ma maîtresse, mes amours*' (*Mémoires d'outre-tombe*, edition of 1949, vol. IV, p. 395f.).

105

Procession of Boats with distant Smoke, Venice
*c.*1845

Oil on canvas; 90 × 120.5 cm

Coll.: Turner Bequest 1856; transferred to the Tate Gallery 1906

The Tate Gallery, London (2068; B/J 505)

Formerly identified as an historical or classical theme, perhaps the burning of Aeneas' ships, it has been suggested that this is more probably a Venetian subject, dating from the mid-1840s. A number of Venetian paintings of this date (some of them unfinished) share technical resemblances with the later watercolours; Turner made use of a white ground as if it were white paper, over which he scattered isolated bursts of bright pigment, creating an effect of brilliant light fragmenting and reflecting colour.

106

Giovanni Antonio Canale, called *Canaletto*
1697–1768

The Bacino on Ascension Day   *c.*1740

Oil on canvas; 121.9 × 182.8 cm

Coll.: In the collection of the Dukes of Leeds, Hornby Castle, probably since the eighteenth century; Duke of Leeds sale, Christie's 11 June 1920 (lot 1), bought A.J. Shelley; bought Lord Revelstoke 1923, by whom bequeathed to the Gallery 1929

Trustees of the National Gallery, London

The most celebrated of all the artists who had painted Venice before Turner, Canaletto was particularly admired in England, where his works had been avidly collected during his lifetime (and where he had come to paint topographical views during the 1740s). Indeed, many English visitors to Venice saw the city through his pictures, like Mrs Piozzi in 1785 for whom the first sight of the city 'revived all the ideas inspired by Canaletti . . . It was wonderfully entertaining to find thus realized all the pleasures that excellent painter had given us'. Turner certainly knew Canaletto's work from drawings and paintings belonging to various patrons as well as from engravings (fig. 18), and his admiration for his predecessor was most clearly demonstrated in the first Venetian oil painting he exhibited, at the Royal Academy in 1833, *Bridge of Sighs . . . Canaletti painting*. The youthful Ruskin, however (in an excess of enthusiasm to prove that Turner was the supreme painter of the city), lamented Canaletto's niggling accuracy, 'what more there is in Venice than brick and stone – what there is of mystery and death, and memory and beauty – what there is to be learned or lamented, to be loved or wept – we look for to Canaletti in vain' (*Works*, III, p. 256); his later writings were to include further savage criticism.

Turner doubtless admired Canaletto's mastery of light and shade, sparkling sense of colour and vivacity of mood, subtlety of composition, and his refusal to be constrained by pedantic considerations of topography. The way in which Canaletto assembled from a mass of carefully observed detail a masterful balance between the actual and the imaginary was an approach which he himself would develop to an infinitely sophisticated degree and infuse with his own genius. For an account of the *Ceremony of the Doge marrying the Sea* see plate 98.

107

Richard Parkes Bonington 1802–1828
The Ducal Palace *c.*1827

Watercolour; 198 × 272 mm

Coll.: Louis Brown, Paris; bought Richard, 4th Marquess of
Hertford; Sir Richard Wallace; Lady Wallace

The Wallace Collection, London (P 656)

Venice's exotic mixture of part-Gothic, part-oriental architecture
made a deep impression on Bonington's romantic imagination. He was
already greatly interested in historical and eastern subject-matter and
an admirer of Byron's poetry – which had inspired his friend
Delacroix's painting *The Execution of Doge Marino Falieri* (Wallace
Collection) – and his visit to Venice in 1826 was to be an important
stimulus for the works of the remaining two years of his life. Besides the
drawings and oil sketches he made of the city's architecture, he also
studied historical costumes in a private collection and pictures in the
Accademia; the rich colouring and invention of the great Venetian
masters like Titian, Tintoretto and Veronese (whose paintings he had
already admired in the Louvre) were to be reflected in his subsequent
figure compositions.

The brilliance and luminosity of Bonington's watercolours inspired
his friends with admiration, if not envy. Delacroix wrote that 'I could
never weary of admiring his marvellous understanding of effects and
the facility of his execution.' This watercolour, based on a pencil
drawing made while he was in Venice, can be dated *c.*1827. The group
of oriental-looking figures in the foreground is characteristic of
Bonington, and gives an extra dimension to an otherwise
straightforward topographical work: one of the figures was based on an
earlier study of the Count of Palatiano in Albanian dress. Bonington
had been given advice on what to see in Venice by Samuel Prout (see
fig. 6), who had visited the city in 1824, but the differences in the two
artists' responses were fundamental. Prout's taste was for picturesquely
quaint architectural detail, while Bonington struck a new, romantic
note.

Although none of Bonington's Venetian watercolours were exhibited
in England during his lifetime, the sale organised in 1829 attracted
much attention and it is almost certain that Turner saw and was
impressed by his works; the influence of the younger artist can be
detected in several paintings and watercolours by Turner of the 1830s.

18. Antonio Visentini after Canaletto, *The Piazzetta: looking North.* After
1743. Engraving.

His first exhibited Venetian oil painting, *Bridge of Sighs . . . Canaletti
painting*, 1833, may partly reflect the example of Bonington, whose
large canvas of *The Ducal Palace* (Tate Gallery, London), exhibited at
the British Institution in January 1828, had been hailed as 'a triumph of
the English School'.

73

108

Richard Parkes Bonington   1802–1828
The Grand Canal   1826

Oil on board; 22.6 × 30.3 cm

Coll.: H.A.J. Munro of Novar; H. Butler Johnstone; Christie's 19
March 1880 (lot 223); Sir W. Cuthbert Quilter sale, Christie's 9 July
1909 (lot 48); George Salting Collection; by descent to Lady
Binning, by whom bequeathed 1952

National Galleries of Scotland, Edinburgh (P(NG) 2164)

Bonington visited Italy in the spring of 1826, accompanied by his
friend and patron Baron Charles Rivet, whose correspondence
described the artist's reactions to the country. They were to spend four
weeks in Venice, Bonington initially in depressed spirits because of
unceasing rain, but, as the weather improved, sketching and drawing
with great application. Unlike Turner, who only rarely made *plein air*
oil studies, relying on numerous rapid pencil drawings, Bonington
made a number of oil sketches in Venice, which he was later to use as
reference for more fully developed paintings. This sketch was the basis
for a painting commissioned in 1827 when Bonington visited London
and found dealers anxious to have Venetian pictures. This commercial
pressure led him to make a number of replicas of the most popular
compositions: a drawing of his Paris *atelier*, made in 1827 by his friend
Thomas Shotter Boys, shows two Venetian subjects in progress – one
of them probably the painting based on this sketch, and the other a
variation in oils of the *Ducal Palace*, plate 107. It was perhaps his
increasing success that led him to attempt a number of large-scale
Venetian subjects, clearly in the style of Canaletto, in the last year of his
life.

   Both this sketch and the finished painting (exhibited at the Royal
Academy in 1828) were subsequently owned by H.A.J. Munro of
Novar, one of Turner's most loyal patrons, in whose collection he
might perhaps have seen them.

109

Clarkson Stanfield   1793–1867
The Dogana   c.1830–1

Watercolour and bodycolour with scratching-out; 220 × 315 mm

Coll.: Henry Vaughan, by whom bequeathed to the Museum 1900

Trustees of the British Museum (1900-8-24-537)

Stanfield's reputation was chiefly as a marine painter, and many of his
contemporaries regarded him as the equal of Turner. During the 1830s
he was one of the foremost contributors to the various illustrated travel
books that had become so popular; Charles Heath's *Picturesque
Annuals* for 1832, 1833 and 1834 were all solely illustrated by
engravings after Stanfield. This watercolour was based on sketches
made during a visit to Venice in 1830 and was engraved by Edward
Goodall (one of Turner's regular engravers) for the *Picturesque Annual*
of 1832. 'The time chosen by the artist is during a storm . . . Woe betide
the Gondoliers that have not time to get home before the riot
commences! . . . all Venice is in an uproar!' Although it is among his
liveliest and most accomplished watercolours, comparison with
Turner's Venetian works shows only too clearly Stanfield's limitations:
an element of melodrama is never far away (it is perhaps worth noting
that he first achieved success as a scene-painter). As Ruskin pointed out
in the first edition of *Modern Painters* I, 1843 (later omitted in the third
edition of 1846) in a discussion of the ways in which artists other than
his hero Turner responded to the city, while Stanfield had feeling for
the truth of architecture and water, yet 'it is all drawn hard and sharp,
there is nothing to hope for or find out, nothing to dream of or discover;
we can measure . . . This cannot be nature, for it is not infinity. No Mr
Stanfield, it is scarcely Venice yet' (*Works*, III, p. 256).

   This watercolour belonged to Henry Vaughan (1809–99) who
owned a number of Turner's Venetian watercolours (see Pls 76, 80, 88,
89, 90, 92, 95).

110

Thomas Moran 1837–1926
S. Maria della Salute 1908

Oil on canvas; 35.6 × 50.8 cm

Signed and dated: *T Moran 1908* and inscribed on the *verso*: *Painted for David Milch, NY T Moran 1908*

Coll.: Acquired from the artist by David Milch; Sotheby Parke-Bernet, New York, 30 May 1984 (lot 4)

Private Collection

Moran's views of Venice show the direct influence of Turner. His first visit to the city was in 1886, but most of his Venetian paintings post-date his second visit, made in 1890. His practice was to make numerous preliminary sketches and watercolours in Venice, but his pictures were painted, exhibited and sold in New York, often appearing side-by-side with his views of the American West. His passion for Venice extended to bringing back to the United States with him in 1890 a gondola said to have been owned by Robert Browning, for use on Hook Pond near his home at East Hampton, Long Island.

His Venetian paintings are characterised by what he himself described as 'dreamy remembrance'; exact topography (as with Turner) was of secondary importance. His works owe much to Turner's paintings (some of which he must have seen in the original, not only in reproduction) in their colouring, lighting, mood and composition.

111

John Singer Sargent 1856–1925
Venice on a grey day: the Riva degli Schiavoni
c.1882

Oil on canvas; 50.8 × 71 cm

Signed and inscribed lower right: *A mon ami Flameng John S Sargent*

Coll.: Sir Philip Sassoon; Miss Hannah Gubbay Bequest to the National Trust 1969

The National Trust

Sargent's earliest visits to Venice were made in 1880 and 1882; this painting shares the silvery-grey tonality and unexpected perspectives of works associated with his second visit. In a letter to a friend written after his return to Paris in December 1882 Sargent noted that 'If you stay there late enough you will perhaps see how curious Venice looks with snow clinging to the roofs and balconies, with a dull sky and the canals a dull opaque green, not unlike pea soup, con rispetto, and very different from the julienne of the Grand Canal in summer' (R. Ormond, *John Singer Sargent*, 1970, p. 30). The picture is dedicated to François Flameng (1856–1923), a popular French painter.

112

Claude Monet 1840–1926
S. Giorgio Maggiore: Sunset 1908

Oil on canvas; 63.5 × 88.9 cm

Signed and dated: *Claude Monet 1908*

Coll.: Bernheim Jeune Gallery, bought from the artist May 1912; Gwendoline Davies, October 1912; bequeathed to the National Museum of Wales 1952

Exh.: Bernheim Jeune Gallery, Paris, *Les 'Venises' de Claude Monet*, 1912, no. 29

National Museum of Wales

Monet's decision to visit Venice in 1908 was perhaps influenced by Turner's paintings of the city, with some of which he had been familiar since his first visit to London in 1870–71. He had apparently been reluctant to visit a city painted by so many earlier artists, but, once he had arrived, he was very much moved by all he saw. At various times he was to admit to a considerable admiration for Turner, an admiration that expressed itself at a profound level, beyond mere stylistic borrowings.

S. Giorgio Maggiore is shown here from the north, the church silhouetted against the sunset sky in the west; the dome of S. Maria della Salute can be seen at the right of the painting.

Paintings of Venetian subjects exhibited by Turner at the Royal Academy 1833–1846

1833 Bridge of Sighs, Ducal Palace and Custom-House, Venice: Canaletti painting (The Tate Gallery, London; B/J 349) *Plate 96*

1833 Ducal Palace, Venice (present whereabouts unknown; B/J 352)

1834 Venice (National Gallery of Art, Washington D.C.; B/J 356)

1835 Venice, from the Porch of Madonna della Salute (The Metropolitan Museum, New York; B/J 362)

1836 Juliet and her Nurse (Sra Amalia Lacroze de Fortabat, Argentina; B/J 365) *Plate 97*

1837 The Grand Canal, Venice (The Huntington Library and Art Gallery, San Marino, California; B/J 368)

1840 Venice, the Bridge of Sighs (The Tate Gallery, London; B/J 383) *Plate 99*

1840 Venice, from the Canale della Giudecca, Chiesa di S. Maria della Salute, &c. (Victoria and Albert Museum, London; B/J 384) *Plate 100*

1841 Ducal Palace, Dogano, with part of San Georgio, Venice (The Allen Memorial Art Museum, Oberlin College, Ohio; B/J 390)

1841 Giudecca, La Donna della Salute and San Georgio (Mr William Wood Prince and the Art Institute of Chicago; B/J 391)

1841 Depositing of John Bellini's Three Pictures in La Chiesa Redentore, Venice (Private Collection; B/J 393)

1842 The Dogano, San Giorgio, Citella, from the Steps of the Europa (The Tate Gallery, London; B/J 396) *Plate 101*

1842 Campo Santo, Venice (The Toledo Museum of Art, Toledo, Ohio; B/J 397) *Plate 102*

1843 The Sun of Venice going to Sea (The Tate Gallery, London; B/J 402) *Plate 103*

1843 Dogana, and Madonna della Salute, Venice (National Gallery of Art, Washington D.C.; B/J 403)

1843 St Benedetto, looking towards Fusina (The Tate Gallery, London; B/J 406)

1844 Venice – Maria della Salute (The Tate Gallery, London; B/J 411)

1844 Approach to Venice (National Gallery of Art, Washington D.C.; B/J 412)

1844 Venice Quay, Ducal Palace (The Tate Gallery, London; B/J 413)

1845 Venice, Evening, going to the Ball (The Tate Gallery, London; B/J 416) *Plate 104*

1845 Morning, returning from the Ball, St. Martino (The Tate Gallery, London; B/J 417)

1845 Venice – Noon (The Tate Gallery, London; B/J 418)

1845 Venice – Sunset, a Fisher (The Tate Gallery, London; B/J 419)

1846 Going to the Ball (San Martino) (Oakpict Inc.; B/J 421)

1846 Returning from the Ball (St Martha) (Oakpict Inc.; B/J 422)

Select Bibliography

Butlin, Martin and Joll, Evelyn, *The Paintings of J.M.W. Turner*, 2 vols, London–New Haven 1977 (2nd edition, revised, 1984)

Butlin, Martin and Wilton, Andrew and Gage, John, *Turner 1775–1851*, exhibition catalogue, Royal Academy, London 1974–5

Clegg, Jeanne, *Ruskin and Venice*, London 1981

Finberg, A.J., *A Complete Inventory of the Drawings of the Turner Bequest*, 2 vols, London 1909

In Venice with Turner, London 1930 (copy in Department of Prints and Drawings, British Museum, with manuscript annotations by C.F. Bell)

The Life of J.M.W. Turner, R.A., 2nd edition, revised and with a supplement by Hilda Finberg, Oxford 1961

George, Hardy, *Turner in Venice*, unpublished Ph.D. thesis, Courtauld Institute of Art, University of London 1970

'Turner in Venice', *Art Bulletin*, vol. LIII, 1971, pp. 84–87

'Turner in Europe in 1833', *Turner Studies*, vol. 4, no. 1, 1984, pp. 2–21

Ginsborg, Paul, *Daniele Manin and the Venetian Revolution of 1848*, Cambridge 1979

Herrmann, Luke, *Ruskin and Turner*, London 1968

Hewison, Robert, *Ruskin and Venice*, London 1978

Honour, Hugh, *The Companion Guide to Venice*, London 1965 (and subsequent editions)

Links, J.G., *Venice for Pleasure*, London 1966 (and subsequent editions)

Lorenzetti, Giulio, *Venezia e il suo Estuario*, Milan 1926 (and subsequent editions 1956, 1961 (in English translation))

Norwich, John Julius, *A History of Venice*, Harmondsworth 1982

Powell, Cecilia, 'Topography, Imagination and Travel: Turner's Relationship with James Hakewill', *Art History*, vol. 5, no. 4, December 1982, pp 408–25

Turner on Classic Ground: his visits to Central and Southern Italy and related paintings and drawings, unpublished Ph.D. thesis, Courtauld Institute of Art, University of London 1985

Rawlinson, W.G., *The Engraved Work of J.M.W. Turner, R.A.*, 2 vols, London 1908, 1913

Ruskin, John, *The Works of John Ruskin*, 39 vols., eds E.T. Cook and Alexander Wedderburn, London 1903–12

Sutton, Anthony and Sutton, Denys, *Venice Rediscovered*, exhibition catalogue, Wildenstein, London 1972

Wilton, Andrew, *Turner in the British Museum: Drawings and Watercolours*, exhibition catalogue, London 1975

The Life and Work of J.M.W. Turner, London 1979

Turner Abroad, London 1982

Zorzi, Alvise, *Venezia Scomparsa*, 2 vols, Venice 1972

The Plates

. . . But let us take, with Turner, the last and greatest step of all. Thank heaven, we are in sunshine again, – and what sunshine! Not the lurid, gloomy, plague-like oppression of Canaletti, but white, flashing fulness of dazzling light, which the waves drink and the clouds breathe, bounding and burning in intensity of joy. That sky, – it is a very visible infinity, – liquid, measureless, unfathomable, panting and melting through the chasms in the long fields of snow-white, flaked, slow-moving vapour, that guide the eye along their multitudinous waves down to the islanded rest of the Euganean hills. Do we dream, or does the white forked sail drift nearer, and nearer yet, diminishing the blue sea between us with the fulness of wings? It pauses now; but the quivering of its bright reflection troubles the shadows of the sea, those azure, fathomless depths of crystal mystery, on which the swiftness of the poised gondola floats double, its black beak lifted like the crest of a dark ocean bird, its scarlet draperies flashed back from the kindling surface, and its bent oar breaking the radiant water into a dust of gold. Dreamlike and dim, but glorious, the unnumbered palaces lift their shafts out of the hollow sea, – pale ranks of motionless flame, – their mighty towers sent up to heaven like tongues of more eager fire, – their grey domes looming vast and dark, like eclipsed worlds, – their sculptured arabesques and purple marble fading farther and fainter, league beyond league, lost in the light of distance. Detail after detail, thought beyond thought, you find and feel them through the radiant mystery, inexhaustible as indistinct, beautiful, but never all revealed; secret in fulness, confused in symmetry, as nature herself is to the bewildered and foiled glance, giving out of that indistinctness, and through that confusion, the perpetual newness of the infinite, and the beautiful.

Yes, Mr. Turner, we are in Venice now.

John Ruskin *Modern Painters* vol. 1 p. 157 1st ed. London 1843

1   On Lake Como   1819

2   S. Giorgio Maggiore: early morning   1819

3   The Punta della Salute, with the Zitelle in the distance: morning   1819

4 Looking east from the Giudecca: early morning (?) 1819

CLXXXI – 7

5   The Campanile of St Mark's and the Ducal Palace   1819

6   The Ducal Palace   *c.*1827

7   The Rialto: moonlight   *c*.1832

8   St Mark's from the Piazzetta   1833?

9   The Piazzetta: night   1833?

10 Moonlight 1833?

11   An open-air theatre (?)   1833?

12   The Campanile of St Mark's from the roof of the Hotel Europa: lightning   1833?

13   The Campanile of St Mark's from the roof of the Hotel Europa: moonlight   1833?

CCCXVIII – 7

14   The interior of St Mark's   1833?

15   The interior of St Mark's   1833?

16   The Dogana from the steps of the Hotel Europa   1833?

17   The Dogana and S. Maria della Salute from the Molo   1833?

18   A procession, perhaps in the Piazza (?)   1833?

19   An interior   1833?

20 The interior of a theatre (?) 1833?

21   The lovers: a scene from 'The Merchant of Venice' (?)   1833?

22 A bridge 1833?

23   A wineshop   1833?

24   The Campanile, from the Atrio of the Palazzo Reale   1833?

CCCXVIII – 38

25 The Ducal Palace: the Porta della Carta 1833?

26 View through medieval arches on to a moonlit canal 1833?

27   The Bridge of Sighs: night   1833?

28   Fireworks on the Molo   1833?

29   S. Maria della Salute: night scene with rockets   1833?

30 The Campanile of St Mark's with the Pilastri Acritani,
from the Porta della Carta   1840?

31   The entrance to the Grand Canal with the Campanile and the Ducal Palace   1840?

32   The Dogana, Campanile of St. Mark's and the Ducal Palace   1840?

33   S. Maria della Salute and the Dogana from the Zitelle, with the Campanile of S. Stefano beyond   1840?

34 The steps of S. Maria della Salute, the Campanile of St Mark's on the left   1840?

CCCXVII – 28

35   S. Giorgio Maggiore with the Dogana   1840?

36   The Grand Canal looking towards the Rialto   1840?

37   View on a cross-canal near the Arsenal (?)   1840?

38   The Grand Canal above the Rialto, with the Ca'd'Oro (?)   1840?

39   The Palazzo Tasca-Papafava   1840?

40   The Ponte della Guerra with the Palazzo Tasca-Papafava beyond   1840?

CCCXVII — 32   41   S. Stefano   1840?

42 A bedroom in Venice 1840?

43   A campanile and other buildings, with a fishing boat   1840?

44   On the Grand Canal looking towards the Rialto   1840?

45   The Grand Canal, with S. Maria della Salute on the left   1840?

46   The Grand Canal, with S. Simeone Piccolo: dusk   1840?

47   Looking down the Grand Canal towards the Casa Corner and S. Maria della Salute   1840?

48   Moonrise, the Giudecca and the Zitelle in the distance   1840?

49   The Giudecca   1840?

50   The Giudecca from the Lagoon   1840?

51   The Giudecca, looking towards Fusina   1840?

52   S. Maria della Salute and the Dogana   1840?

53   S. Maria della Salute and the Dogana: sunset   1840?

54   On the Grand Canal   1840?

55 The Rialto, the Palazzo Balbi on the left 1840?

56   From my Bedroom, Venice   1840?

57   A distant view of the entrance to the Grand Canal   1840?

58   S. Maria della Salute with the Traghetto S. Maria Zobenigo   1840?

59 S. Maria della Salute, the Campanile of St Mark's, the Ducal Palace and S. Giorgio Maggiore from the Giudecca 1840?

60   The Rialto, from the Riva del Carbon   after 1818

61   On the Giudecca looking towards Fusina   1840?

62   S. Maria della Salute, the Campanile and S. Giorgio Maggiore from the Canale della Grazia   1840?

63   The Ducal Palace and the Riva degli Schiavoni   1840?

64   The Riva degli Schiavoni from the channel to the Lido   1840?

65   The Riva degli Schiavoni, from near S. Biagio   1840?

66   The Ducal Palace from the Dogana   1840?

67   Shipping off the Riva degli Schiavoni, from near the Ponte dell'Arsenale   1840?

68   S. Giorgio Maggiore and S. Maria della Salute: calm at sunrise   1840?

69   The Riva degli Schiavoni   1840?

70   The approach to Venice: sunset   1840?

71   The Ponte della Pietà on the Riva degli Schiavoni   1840?

72   The Ponte Ca'di Dio (?)   1840?

73   The Grand Canal, looking towards the Dogana   1840?

74   View from the roof of the Hotel Europa   1833 or 1840?

75   The Arsenal   1840?

76   S. Giorgio Maggiore (?)   1840?

77   S. Giorgio Maggiore at sunset from the Hotel Europa   1840?

78   S. Giorgio Maggiore from the Dogana   1840?

79   The Lagoon, behind S. Giorgio Maggiore (?)   1840?

80   The Grand Canal   1840?

81 Moonlight 1840?

82   St Mark's and the Ducal Palace   1840?

83 Venice from Fusina (?) 1840?

84   S. Giorgio Maggiore and the Zitelle from the Giudecca   1840?

85   Looking eastward towards the Campanile of St Mark's: sunrise (?)   1840?

86   A storm at sunset   1840?

87 A storm on the Lagoon 1840?

88   A storm in the Piazzetta   1840?

89   Venice from the Lagoon   1840?

90   The Piazzetta and the Ducal Palace   1840?

91   The Accademia   1840?

92   S. Maria della Salute, from the Canal   1840?

93 The Grand Canal, looking towards S. Maria della Salute 1840?

94   The Grand Canal, with S. Maria della Salute   *c.*1840

95 The Sun of Venice 1840?

96   Bridge of Sighs, Ducal Palace and Custom-House, Venice: Canaletti painting   1833

97 Juliet and her Nurse 1836

98   Venice, the Piazzetta with the Ceremony of the Doge marrying the sea   *c.*1835

99   Venice, the Bridge of Sighs   1840

100   Venice, from the Canale della Giudecca, Chiesa di S. Maria della Salute, &c   1840

101   The Dogano, San Giorgio, Citella, from the Steps of the Europa   1842

102   Campo Santo, Venice   1842

103   The Sun of Venice going to sea   1843

104   Venice, Evening, going to the Ball   1845

105   Procession of Boats with distant Smoke, Venice   *c*.1845

106   *Giovanni Antonio Canale* called *Canaletto* (1697–1768)   The Bacino on Ascension Day   *c.*1740

107 *Richard Parkes Bonington* (1802–1828) The Ducal Palace *c.*1827

108 *Richard Parkes Bonington* (1802–1828)   The Grand Canal   1826

109   *Clarkson Stanfield* (1793–1867)   The Dogana   *c.*1830–31

110   *Thomas Moran* (1837–1926)   S. Maria della Salute   1908

111 *John Singer Sargent* (1856–1925)   Venice on a grey day: the Riva degli Schiavoni   *c*.1882

112 *Claude Monet* (1840–1926)   S. Giorgio Maggiore: sunset   1908